REINSURAN
LONDON MARKET

PRACTICAL INSURANCE GUIDES

Titles in this series are:

How to Manage Risk
2nd edition
by Jim Bannister

Insurance Solvency Analysis
2nd edition
by Jim Bannister

Introduction to Insurance
2nd edition
by D S Hansell

Professional Negligence and Insurance Law
by Neil F Jones & Co

Reinsurance: London Market Practice
by Carol Boland

Reinsurance Management
by Leslie Lucas, John McLean and Peter Green

The Nuts and Bolts of Reinsurance
by Keith Riley

REINSURANCE: LONDON MARKET PRACTICE

BY

CAROL BOLAND

LLP

LONDON HONG KONG

1996

LLP Professional Publishing
69-77 Paul Street
London EC2A 4LQ

EAST ASIA
LLP Asia
Sixth Floor
233 Hollywood Road
Hong Kong

First published in 1993 as *Reinsurance Office Practice*
This edition published 1996
Reprinted 1999

British Library Cataloguing in Publication Data
A catalogue record for this book
is available from the British Library

ISBN 1-85978-580-8

LLP Professional Publishing is a trading division of Informa Publishing Group Limited

Text set in 10 on 12pt Plantin by
Interactive Sciences Ltd, Gloucester
Printed in Great Britain by
WBC Ltd
Bridgend, Mid-Glamorgan

PREFACE

My intention in writing this book on reinsurance office procedures in the London Market is to provide a quick introduction/reference for those wishing to find out more about the ever-changing face of underwriting and accounting systems in the non-marine company market. I say a "quick reference", as the book does not presume to be in any way a reinsurance Bible, and assumes that the reader has some understanding of the various terms used throughout. The changing shape of the London reinsurance market, together with the accompanying developments in technology, is keeping all those involved in reinsurance constantly on their toes. Even as I write, I am aware of further proposals for streamlining existing systems.

However, I remain undeterred by this changing reinsurance environment and trust that what follows provides a starting point for those wishing to keep up with current London Market practice. There are a number of people to whom I am grateful for giving me their time and assistance in compiling this book and, without naming names, they include various people at: LPC, Greig Fester Ltd., LIMNET, ILU, Citibank N.A. (London), Mendes & Mount (New York), Compre Administrators, Scan Reinsurance Company Ltd. and, of course, LLP.

August 1996 CAROL BOLAND

THE AUTHOR

Carol Boland has spent over 20 years in the insurance industry, working in both Dublin and London. In 1977 she first entered the world of reinsurance as a trainee company underwriter, and was one of the handful of pioneering women trainees in the London Market at that time.

In 1990 Carol resigned her position as International Excess of Loss and Proportional Treaty Underwriter with a London reinsurance company, to set up Reinsurance Project Management Ltd., a reinsurance consultancy and training company. In addition, she has also established herself as an insurance journalist and author, writing regularly for prominent reinsurance publications in London.

A Fellow of the Chartered Insurance Institute and a Chartered Insurer, Carol is also a member of the Association of Insurance Teachers (AIT).

CONTENTS

LIST OF FIGURES

CHAPTER 1

WHAT IS REINSURANCE?

"Man owes his success to his creativity. No one doubts the need for it. It is more useful in good times and essential in bad." (EDWARD DEBONO, *Lateral Thinking for Management*)

WHAT IS REINSURANCE?

Is reinsurance really necessary?

This may seem a strange question to pose at the start of a book on reinsurance practice; it is, however, one worth considering. The idea that, fundamentally, insurance operations need to purchase reinsurance is a concept that should, and in some cases must, be viewed with an open mind.

However, there can be no reinsurance without insurance, and understanding the principles of insurance is a prerequisite to understanding the principles of reinsurance. So, the history of the development of insurance seems like a good place to begin an account of reinsurance practice.

The history of reinsurance is brief when set against the annals of insurance, as insurance in a non-commercial form has existed as long as the recognition of risk itself; parents insuring against infirmity in old age through their children, and family units joining together into larger protective groups to form a society.

By the sixteenth century the practice of insurance became well established among the shipping merchants of the day, and the increasing volume of trade in the seventeenth century led to the establishment of the first professional insurers. Much of the insurance business of the day was carried out at Mr Lloyd's coffee shop in London, where the establishment acted as a central meeting place where many of the merchants gathered to discuss maritime matters.

Indeed, it was Mr Lloyd's coffee shop which provided the site for the first insurance market situated under one roof. This single market lives on in the guise of Lloyd's, which, up to the introduction of corporate insurers, followed the tradition of individuals as insurers of risks.

With the advancement of capitalism in the late eighteenth century and the onset of the Industrial Revolution, many new threats and risks to capital were evident. So it was that the nineteenth century saw the rapid development of non-marine insurance as the demand for cover increased and insurance became a profitable line of business.

THE DEVELOPMENT OF REINSURANCE

The development of a reinsurance market took a rockier road. Reinsurance of marine risks is thought to be as old as commercial insurance, but it was not until 1864 that the practice in the UK was legalised and the ban on marine reinsurance was removed. Previously, reinsurance had been considered as a form of gambling.

As reinsurance of fire business appeared unattractive to UK insurers, co-insurance remained a more common way of spreading the risk. Insurers wishing to spread their risks then had to turn to the continental merchant banks for their reinsurance protection.

It was in continental Europe, in the early 1800s, that automatic treaty reinsurance was first developed and there are numerous examples on record of facultative and treaty reinsurance arrangements at that time.

However, it took until 1852 for the first independent reinsurance company to be established, and that company was the Ruchversicherrungs Gesellschaft of Cologne. Several German companies, including the Aachener Ruck, followed suit, proving themselves to be as productive as their forerunner. Unfortunately, British reinsurers who decided to enter the field found that their initial experiences were not so fortuitous.

In the 1870s, quite soon after setting up, a number of UK reinsurance companies went into liquidation. The reasons for their lack of success are not altogether clear, but the UK retained its role as a modest reinsurance market for some time, with its European counterparts continuing to hold the stronger market position.

It is in 1880 that we find the earliest trace of excess of loss reinsurance, as established by Mr Cuthbert Heath of Lloyd's, and not until 1907 do we find the establishment of Britain's oldest and longest operating reinsurance company, the Mercantile and General.

Then came the First World War, which brought with it a curtailment in trading relationships between the UK and its primary reinsurance markets. This forced companies to look within their own national boundary for cover and Lloyd's, a late entrant to the reinsurance market, began to take a more active role, attracting a large volume of business from the United States of America.

By the end of the Second World War London had successfully established itself at the heart of the international reinsurance market. The City of London had become the centre for reinsurance capacity and expertise, with capital provided by British and overseas companies and also those many individuals who were members at Lloyd's.

Other reinsurance markets overseas, particularly in Germany and the United States, continued to develop their major domestic reinsurance markets and many of these overseas companies set up branches and contact offices in the London market where they provided, as they still do, a large part of the reinsurance capacity available in London.

What is this business of reinsurance?

In a few words it may be described as the passing on of all or part of a risk by one insuring party to another. Or, put another way, the business of insuring the insurers.

Reinsurance is essentially, though not exclusively, an international business. It is "essentially" so because the widest spreading of risk is fundamental to the character of reinsurance.

With any portfolio of risks the law of large numbers can only apply where there are an indefinite number of identical risks. As this cannot be the case, insurers will always operate under an imperfect application of the law. The limitations in applying the law of large numbers and the desirability of spreading the risk for an insurer are just as relevant to a prudent reinsurer.

The reason why reinsurance is purchased is, fundamentally, to reduce the degree to which claims fluctuate from those expected. A list of reasons to purchase reinsurance may look something like this:

Reinsurance may be purchased to:

- Protect the financial stability of insurers from adverse underwriting results.
- Stabilise claims ratios from one year to the next.
- Minimise claims accumulation from losses within and between different classes.
- Geographically spread the risk.
- Increase capacity.
- Increase the profitability of insurers through permitting greater flexibility in the size and types of risk accepted.
- Secure technical support and help.

As reinsurers also purchase reinsurance, or retrocession cover, these arguments for purchasing cover may also apply to reinsurers.

Insurers may also require additional services provided by reinsurers, such as expertise help in the rating of large risks which are outside their technical capabilities. This service can be particularly important to a small insurer operating in a developing country.

Established reinsurers may also be of assistance in the training of reinsurance personnel in areas such as underwriting, claims and technical processing.

METHODS AND TYPES OF REINSURANCE

There are two main methods by which insurance business may be reinsured:

- proportional, and
- non-proportional.

Proportional reinsurance business is a method by which all premiums and losses on a risk or portfolio of risks are shared proportionately.

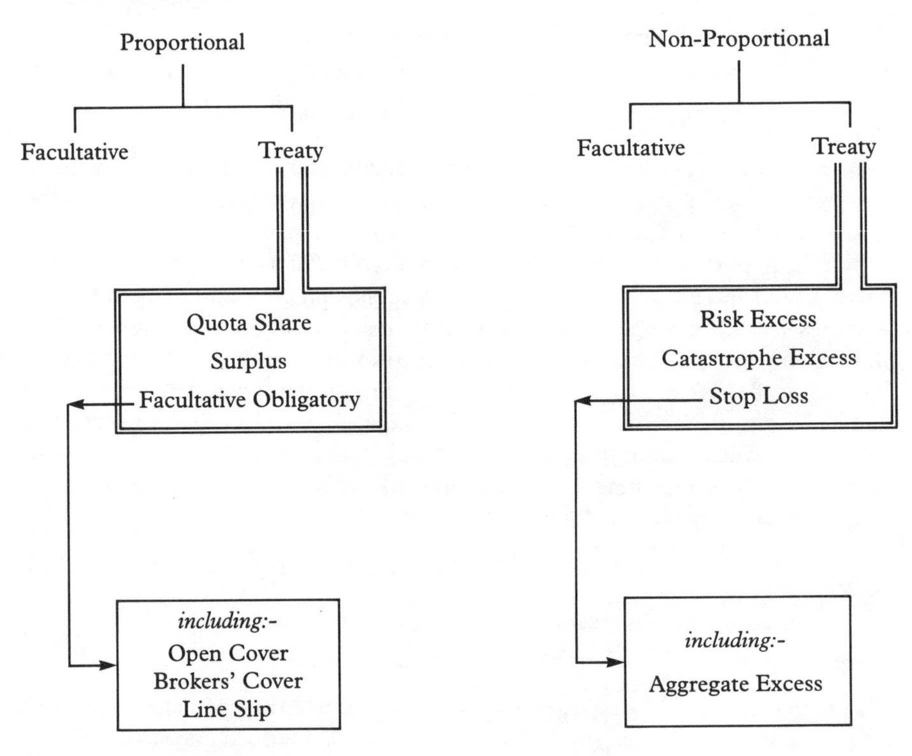

Figure 1: methods of reinsurance

Non-proportional reinsurance is where the reinsurers agree to pay for losses above, or in excess of, a certain amount, up to an agreed limit, in return for a predetermined premium.

Within each of these two methods of reinsurance there are two main types of reinsurance:

- facultative, and
- treaty.

The various types of facultative and treaty reinsurances shown in Figure 1, Methods of Reinsurance, are now considered.

Facultative

Facultative policies are the original and simplest form of cover for individual risks. The cedant has the choice whether or not to purchase reinsurance and reinsurers have the freedom to decline the risk. Facultative obligatory treaties, discussed later, are often written in the facultative department because of this freedom of choice in the ceding of risks. Facultative protection may be of a proportional or non-proportional nature.

Sum Insured	:	$100,000,000
Primary policy	:	$ 10,000,000*
1st Layer	:	$ 10,000,000 xs $ 10,000,000
2nd Layer	:	$ 20,000,000 xs $ 20,000,000
3rd Layer	:	$ 60,000,000 xs $ 40,000,000

* Including Reinsured's Retention

The premium for each layer, or policy, is sometimes expressed as a percentage of the original net premium (ONP) received by the reinsured for the whole risk.

Figure 2: a facultative reinsurance programme

Proportional

This is the method by which individual risks or a schedule of risks under one policy are reinsured. The original premium and deductions and losses are all split proportionally between the reinsured and the reinsurers. The reinsured's participation or share of the risk is termed a retention.

The policy may be issued on a total sum insured basis (TSI) or a probable maximum loss basis (PML) or on a first loss basis. A first loss policy, or primary insurance, usually covers a schedule of risks for an amount less than the top risk value, say the first 10 per cent. The remainder of the risk values may be covered by facultative excess of loss policies.

Non-proportional

Excess of loss cover became popular as risk values increased and insurers felt obliged to write larger lines to keep competitors at bay. In its simplest form, the insurer accepts 100 per cent of the risk, decides on a suitable amount to retain and reinsures any losses which are in excess of the retained amount. The excess amount can then be split into a number of different layered policies, with each policy sitting above the underlying policy layer, see Figure 2.

Treaty

To overcome the high administration costs and uncertainty of reinsuring large numbers of individual risks on a facultative basis, the reinsurance treaty came into being.

Proportional treaties include quota shares, various levels of surpluses and facultative obligatory treaties. Non-proportional treaties include risk excess of losses, catastrophe excess of losses, stop losses and aggregate excesses.

A proportional treaty may be referred to as a pro-rata or surplus lines or excess lines treaty. A non-proportional treaty may be referred to as an excess of loss, excess or X/L treaty or contract.

The party passing on liability may be termed the cedant, insured, reinsured or retrocedant and the party accepting the liability may be termed the reinsurer or retrocessionaire. Apart from the term cedant, which can be applied to all parties passing on liability, the terminology used depends on where the party is in the chain of reinsurance buying and selling.

Proportional

Quota share treaties operate by the reinsured ceding an agreed percentage of all gross acceptances on agreed class(es) of business. Premiums and losses are shared on a proportional basis and the reinsured must cede, and reinsurers must accept, all risks which fall within the scope of the treaty. The retention and quota share cession may be termed the gross retention.

Surplus treaties receive risks with sum insureds over the reinsured's gross retention. Each risk is ceded on a proportional basis with reinsurers receiving a pro-rata share of the full risk premium and paying a share of every claim on the risk. The cession to the treaty is expressed in terms of lines, with one line equalling the reinsured's retention.

The treaty cession is limited to a maximum number of lines either on a gross line basis, including quota share reinsurers' capacity, or a net line basis, excluding said reinsurances.

A number of surplus treaties may be purchased to build up the sum insured capacity needed to write larger risks. Usually, no more than three treaties are purchased, the second and subsequent treaties receiving a share of the risk once the underlying treaties have received a cession. Each treaty receiving a cession will pay its proportionate share of each loss occurring on that risk, regardless of the size of the loss.

Facultative obligatory treaties combine features of both the facultative and treaty methods of proportional reinsurance. The reinsured is not compelled to cede risks to the treaty but, when a cession is correctly made, reinsurers must accept the liability. Fac/obligs, as the treaties are often called, may be lined or unlined. Other treaties which may also be included in the facultative underwriters' portfolio of risks, are

- Open covers which operate in the same way as Fac/obligs but tend to be unlined. There is, therefore, no relationship between the amount ceded and the reinsured's retention on the risk.
- Brokers' covers which are another form of Fac/obligs, where the reinsurers must accept the risks ceded to the treaty. The difference is that risks are bound by the broker rather than the reinsured. Brokers

operate the cover without of course participating in the risk and take a commission for their services.

— Line slips which are virtually the same as brokers' covers except risks cannot be bound by the broker and risks must be submitted to the leading reinsurer(s) for binding. Following reinsurers are obliged to accept the risks bound.

All proportional treaties are facilities which grant underwriters additional capacity with which to attract business.

Non-proportional

Treaty reinsurance on a non-proportional, or excess of loss basis, covers losses on a portfolio of risks. Contracts are placed in layers in the same manner as described for a facultative excess. The layers normally cover the reinsureds' net retention but may also include, if required, liability of proportional reinsurers.

There are two basic forms of cover:

- Per risk
- Per event.

Per risk

A risk excess, as the name implies, is designed to cover risk losses over a set amount of excess point. The reinsured determines a suitable level of loss retention and all losses above that amount are recoverable from the risk excess(es). The excess amount may be placed in one or several layers and recoveries per layer are normally limited by reinstatements to an overall maximum liability in any one period and/or occurrence.

Per event

Catastrophe excesses, or cat x/ls, cover losses involving more than one risk. In the event of a large loss from one occurrence, say a windstorm, the company may find itself subject to an accumulation of separate risk losses on its net retention. The cedant calculates the amount of loss it can withstand from one event without jeopardising its solvency position and reinsures loss amounts above this figure.

A layered catastrophe programme may cover one specific account or a number of different classes of account. A specific programme relates to particular account(s), for example a satellite account, whereas a whole account programme covers a whole range of accounts, including those under the specific protection(s). Often the reinsured is required to retain a percentage of each layer—5 per cent or 10 per cent is the norm. As with risk excesses, the reinsured's maximum recovery in any one year is normally limited by reinstatement provisions. If a frequency of claims is expected, the layers may be termed "workers" or "working" layers.

Stop loss protections cover the accumulation of net losses in any one year after taking into account all other recoveries on proportional and excess of loss protections. They are issued on an excess of loss basis where the limit and excess are expressed as a percentage of the reinsured's gross or net income in a 12-month period. The protection can be placed in a number of layers.

An aggregate excess is basically the same type of cover as a stop loss protection except the limit and excess points are expressed as a monetary amount as opposed to a percentage of income. Also, an aggregate excess tends to cover specific perils, e.g. storm, as opposed to protecting the full range of whole account perils.

Examples of the slip details on a facultative, surplus and catastrophe excess of loss placement are shown in Appendices 1, 2 and 3, at the back of this book.

A reinsurance programme

A reinsurance programme refers to the total reinsurance protections purchased by a cedant and, if the market is buoyant, the programme may well include a quota share treaty, a first surplus, a risk excess and several layers of catastrophe protection.

Figure 3 shows how a reinsurance programme may be set up to cover two underwriting accounts A and B, within the same reinsurance company. In the example both accounts are separately protected by various types of proportional reinsurances and specific excesses. The cedant's retentions are accumulated for recovery under the catastrophe excesses for losses arising from the same event.

The final stop loss reinsurance protects the annual aggregate losses on both accounts, after all other reinsurances.

For practical examples on how to underwrite various types of reinsurances, reference should be made to R. Kiln's book, *Reinsurance Underwriting*.

THE MARKET PLACE

Reinsurance markets may be likened to clearing houses where buyers and sellers of reinsurance negotiate risk transfer. The negotiations are carried out direct with clients or through a reinsurance broker and, as with all markets, the price of the commodity fluctuates and is subject to market forces.

The market forces which influence the price transfer are determined by a number of factors, but predominately by supply and demand. Where demand is greater than supply the price of reinsurance tends to increase and, conversely, where the supply is greater than the demand the price tends to fall.

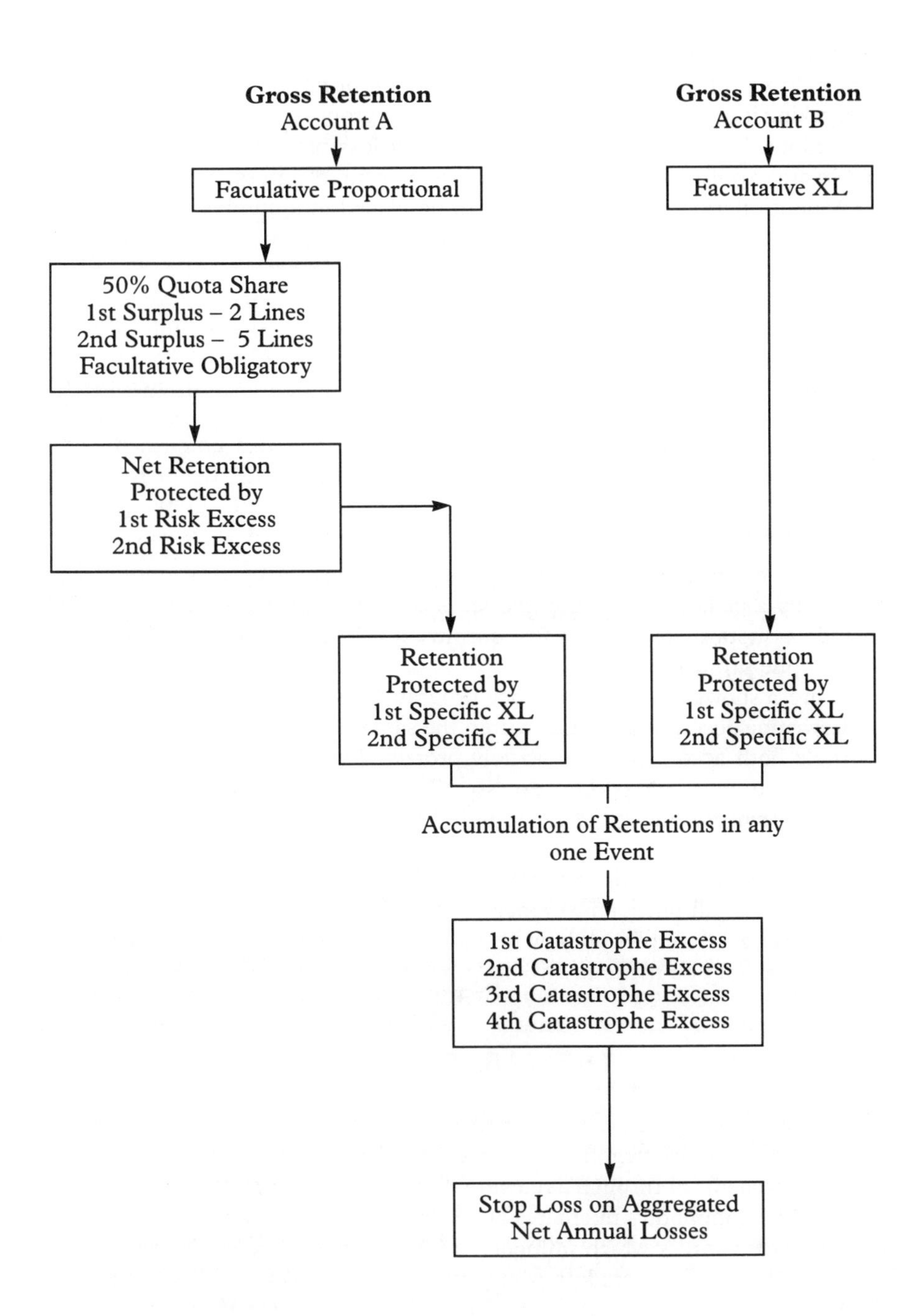

Figure 3: a reinsurance programme

The supply of reinsurance is influenced by such factors as the comparative profitability of alternative business investments or a company's need to expand its market share. The biggest influence on supply is, of course, the ability to make money for investors.

Reinsurance demand, however, is strongly linked to price. The more competitive the cost of reinsurance protection, the more attractive is the option to reinsure as opposed to retaining the risk in-house.

As with all markets, the reinsurance market is made up of buyers and sellers, with brokers, or intermediaries, playing a major role in bringing all parties together.

Other participants that also form an important part of the market include reinsurance consultants, accounting bureaux, trade associations, financial analysts, lawyers and accountants, together making the reinsurance market what it is today.

Who are the buyers and sellers of reinsurance? There is no clear dividing line between who buys and who sells reinsurance; indeed, a reinsurance operation is often both a buyer and seller of reinsurance. Looking at the London reinsurance market we see the types of buyer and seller who operate throughout the world:

- — Professional reinsurance companies
- — Lloyd's syndicates
- — Direct insurance companies
- — Underwriting agencies
- — State reinsurance corporation.

Buyers of reinsurance

Most operations which write insurance or reinsurance business tend also to be buyers of some form of reinsurance protection.

As one would suspect, direct insurers are the main buyers who may deal direct with other insurers or reinsurers and/or through one or more reinsurance brokers. State insurance corporations and captive insurance companies are also major buyers of reinsurance and mainly look to the international broker to spread their risk.

Lloyd's syndicates tend to buy reinsurance from other syndicates, largely due to the rules which encourage this choice. However, a good proportion of their reinsurance needs are met by companies in London and overseas.

Reinsurers of direct insurers also purchase reinsurance cover from other reinsurance companies in the retrocession market. These companies in turn may purchase retrocession cover from fellow reinsurance companies and it is in this way that the so-called "spiral" losses are generated in the retrocession market. For example, reinsurer A buys cover from reinsurer B, who in turn buys cover from reinsurer C, who in turn buys cover from reinsurers A and B. So, the same loss may be repeatedly passed between the same reinsurers until, in some cases, the level of cover purchased is exhausted and further loss payments are retained net.

Sellers of reinsurance

Sellers of reinsurance include direct insurance companies through their reinsurance divisions, reinsurance companies, Lloyd's syndicates, underwriting agencies and state reinsurance corporations.

Sellers usually price reinsurance in line with market trends, though the price of reinsurance can vary quite a bit between reinsurers. Some follow the market's highs and lows when rating, while others take a more consistent view of the rating process. There are a number of sophisticated tools which many underwriters use in their rating procedure, including computer modules based on catastrophe exposures and accumulations within a territory.

Most sellers appreciate that price is not the only factor which influences buyers and that other elements, such as the degree of sound security offered, also play an important part in determining the attractiveness of a price. Indeed, the spate of companies which have ceased actively underwriting has made the whole reinsurance market aware of the importance of reinsuring with sound, long-term security.

Reinsurance brokers

Reinsurance brokers, or intermediaries, have an important bearing on the activities within the reinsurance market as they help to bring together the buyer and seller within national and across international boundaries. Brokers may be divided into two main groups:

- Lloyd's brokers
- Non-Lloyd's brokers.

A Lloyd's broker is approved by the Corporation of Lloyd's to transact business directly with Lloyd's syndicates, whereas the non-Lloyd's broker is not. Lloyd's approval means that the broker has met certain standards or criteria as regards the running of their broking operation.

Brokers vary in size and shape. There are the giant international brokers with offices worldwide who advise on all aspects and classes of reinsurance and have much influence in the various reinsurance markets. At the other end of the scale, though becoming less common, is the niche or specialist broker who concentrates on limited classes or areas of reinsurance.

The main services provided by reinsurance brokers may be summarised as follows:

- Acquisition and placing of business
- The servicing of existing business
- Risk management and other consultancy services.

The acquisition and placing of business involves establishing lines of communication with appropriate underwriters. Brokers are expected to "know the market" and in London this is relatively easy, but for those brokers operating outside such a concentrated market much travelling is necessary. Although perhaps 80 per cent of proportional treaty business is traded direct, brokers still play a major role in the placing of non-proportional business, and have firmly proven the importance of their role in reinsurance negotiations.

The services demanded of brokers differ from one client to another. Their advice may be sought on how to set up a reinsurance operation or, further along the line, guidance may be required on the level of reinsurance that should be purchased or on how their reinsurance programme should be structured.

As regards contract negotiations, a broker's advice may be required at the initial stage when terms and conditions are being discussed and agreed with the market. Alternatively, some brokers' services may only be required after the contract has been quoted and led off.

Brokers may also act as agents of reinsurers through the operation of an underwriting agency. Here they may accept risks on behalf of underwriters, under an agency agreement, or, on a smaller scale, under a specific binding authority.

Other major services which brokers perform include the collection of premiums and the servicing and co-ordination of claim settlements and the drawing up of contract wordings.

Product development, in conjunction with leading reinsurers, is another important part of the brokers' role, and an essential one if new business is to be attracted into the London Market.

Some brokers have built up their expertise in risk management and the management of captive insurance companies. Here, their role is often one of consultancy and of advising clients on the most effective way to organise their insurances.

In the London Market, brokers take a keen interest in the total development and operation of their home market and liaise with reinsurers and London Market associations, through the Lloyd's Insurance Brokers Committee —LIBC. The committee represents about 220 brokers who together employ over 55,000 staff and generate a total brokerage income in the region of £2.5 billion a year.

METHODS OF PLACEMENT

The way in which reinsurance is placed depends on whether the cedant wishes to place the business direct with reinsurers and/or employs the services of a reinsurance broker.

In London the tradition of the broker walking the risk around the market, with placing slip and information to hand, is still the main method of risk placement by brokers.

Those reinsurers based outside the London Market are offered business by London and other international brokers by way of post and fax. Faxes have almost replaced telexes and, to a great extent, postal offers.

However, the use of electronic networks, such as LIMNET and RINET, for transmitting offers of business, is rapidly gaining momentum. Electronic offers may currently be sent by electronic mail (E-mail) or via the Electronic Placing Support system (EPS). EPS is an electronic system which uses an electronic slip, or E-slip, for the offer and acceptance or declining of risks, and it is considered by many to be the method which will substantially replace all other methods of risk placement, both in London and eventually worldwide.

The system is currently in operation between brokers and underwriters in the London Market, and placement targets, using this method, are in force to actively encourage London brokers to use the system.

It is felt unlikely that the initial face-to-face negotiations between slip leader and broker will be eliminated by the introduction of the E-slip; however, for those following underwriters offered a share of the risk, the current system of face-to-face negotiations, in the future, may prove to be the exception rather than the rule.

The everyday use of video phones by London reinsurers, as an aid to risk placement, is still a long way off. But, as more business is transacted electronically, video phones may well become popular, permitting a form of "face-to-face" broking to continue.

Those cedants placing business direct with their reinsurers use complementary methods of placement, and direct links may be established between the two contracting parties through representatives who regularly travel to potential client markets. Here the traveller may set up reciprocal exchanges of business or establish a line of communication for future business offers.

Companies wishing to deal direct may also use the electronic networks to communicate, using the electronic mail systems (E-mail) as previously mentioned.

In summary, Figure 4 shows the possible paths a cedant's offer of reinsurance may take, using traditional and/or electronic methods of placement.

Although the placing methods for reinsurance business have remained largely unchanged over the past 50 years, these long-established methods are currently subject to dramatic restyling. The pressure is now on both brokers and reinsurers to move forward using the E-slip as a more efficient and cost effective way to do business.

AGREEING THE TERMS

Following on from risk placement, the terms of a reinsurance contract may be agreed direct between the contracting parties or with the intervention of a broker.

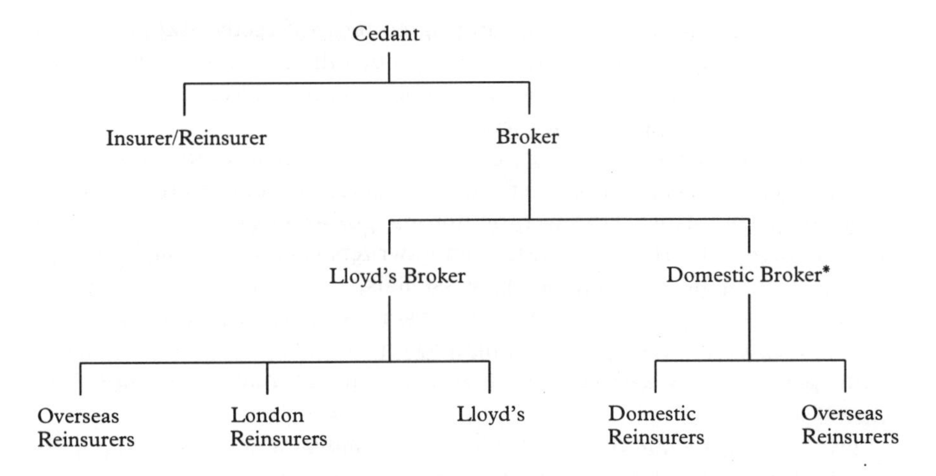

* "*Domestic*" is the term used to describe a broker or reinsurer based within the cedant's home country.

Figure 4: placement flow chart

Brokers have probably played their biggest role in the negotiating of excess of loss terms and conditions. The final terms are often agreed after lengthy negotiations between the two contracting parties, with the broker acting as intermediary.

The offer and acceptance process in the London Market may go something like this:

Cedant contacts London broker to arrange meeting

↓

Broker and cedant discuss reinsurance requirements

↓

Broker advises cedant and draws up quotation slip

↓

Broker visits leading underwriters and obtains terms

↓

Broker contacts cedant for further discussions

↓

Cedant accepts terms and gives broker firm order

↓

Broker returns to lead underwriter for line on slip

↓

Broker continues placement until slip order completed.

In cases where cedant and reinsurer agree terms directly, the process of offer, counter-offer and final acceptance, is much the same. The relationship between the two parties tends, however, to be a closer one as personal contact is maintained over a number of years.

In reciprocal proportional treaty exchanges, each reinsurer may be subject to unique terms and conditions, reflecting the quality of reinsurance offered in this exchange of treaties. However, on non-reciprocal business, the practice of different slips and terms for different underwriters is viewed as an unacceptable practice by most reinsurance professionals.

Many factors are taken into account when a cedant decides which alternative quotation to accept, price being only one; reputation of leader, leader's claims paying ability and likelihood of continuity on renewal are also very important.

Once the terms of the contract are finalised and the contract fully placed the offer details become the basis for drawing up a full contract wording.

CHAPTER 2

THE REINSURANCE MARKETS

"There are few ways in which a man can be more innocently employed than getting money." (SAMUEL JOHNSON, 1709–1784)

The existence of a market does not require the presence of buyers and sellers in one particular building or area; the main criterion for its successful operation is that traders can communicate to transact business. It could be said that there is really only one reinsurance market, that is the worldwide market. According to a Swiss Reinsurance study, the worldwide demand for reinsurance in 1992 was some $150bn (£100bn), with the top 10 markets accounting for three quarters of the total. The US remains by far the biggest purchaser at $43.3bn, followed by Germany at $23.8bn and the UK at $16.4bn.

The reinsurance market(s) operate in a constantly changing environment. What makes a risk attractive to reinsurers today, may make it unattractive tomorrow and tax regulations, accounting and legal processes all have an effect on reinsurers' attitude to risk.

As one market contracts, another expands, taking up the surplus capacity which over-spills and, with the current harmonising of EU insurance and reinsurance regulations, this may also bring about further changes which will influence reinsurers' future business strategies.

THE REINSURANCE MARKETS

The five main international trading areas, or markets, which are now discussed, are:

- The United Kingdom
- The Continent of Europe
- The United States of America
- The Far East
- Offshore.

The United Kingdom

The London Market

London is an international centre for the placing of protections for insurance and reinsurance companies throughout the world. It has a reputation for the strength of its security and its innovative style of underwriting, leading the way in electronic risk placement and electronic claim advice and settlement systems.

The London Market's underwriting resources are produced by Lloyd's and the company market, and in 1992 the total market generated a gross premium income of approximately £10.8bn (Swiss Re Study); 52 per cent was written by companies and P&I clubs and 48 per cent by Lloyd's. The uniqueness of the Lloyd's operation and the position of the surrounding reinsurance companies is considered to have made London the major reinsurance centre it is today.

Lloyd's

The Lloyd's market is housed at 1, Lime Street, in the heart of the City.

The Corporation of Lloyd's provides a market place for over 14,000 individuals called "Names" or "underwriting members" and these Names are personally liable for policyholders' claims for unlimited amounts of liability. From 1994, incorporated Names, with limited liability, were admitted to Lloyd's in a move to attract further capital into the insurance market and in 1995 there were over 120 corporate Names in existence. However, the number of active syndicates has greatly reduced over recent years through closures and mergers, and in 1995 they had reduced to approximately 180 in number.

Syndicates are formed to accept risks, using the services of a professional underwriter, and are backed by a collection of Names. Names who work within the Lloyd's system are known as "working Names", and those with no such direct working links are termed "external Names".

The market is served by Lloyd's registered brokers and underwriting and members' agents. The agents provide services to syndicates and members.

There are a number of underwriting associations to which underwriters may belong. Based on classes of business, they include:

Lloyd's Underwriters' Association (LUA), for marine underwriters
Lloyd's Underwriters Non-Marine Association (NMA)
Lloyd's Aviation Underwriters' Association (LAUA)
Lloyd's Motor Underwriters' Association (LMUA).

Lloyd's is a self-regulatory body and is controlled by the Council of Lloyd's, and it is continuing to experience a process of change and reorganisation, including the implementation of many of the recommendations set out in the Lloyd's Task Force report, published in January 1992, and the subsequent Lloyd's Business Plan.

Companies

The London company market is concentrated in the City of London, in proximity to the Lloyd's building. It constitutes roughly half of the total

London market capacity through more than 100 UK and foreign-owned corporate insurers. The market is broadly divided into marine and non-marine underwriters, though certain companies underwrite both classes of business.

The development of two market underwriting centres, the Institute of London Underwriters (ILU), for marine and aviation risks, and the London Underwriting Centre (LUC), for mainly non-marine risks, are evidence of the changing face of the company market. These centres aim, *inter alia*, to provide brokers with more speedy access to company underwriters who were previously scattered around the market.

The Department of Trade and Industry (DTI) regulates the operation of insurance and reinsurance companies in the UK, and Lloyd's, globally.

For regulation purposes, companies are split into:

— companies incorporated in the UK
— branches of companies incorporated in other EU member states
— branches of companies incorporated outside the EU.

The first type of company listed includes subsidiaries of foreign companies, which make up the majority of reinsurance companies in this category. The second and third types of company include "contact" offices. Contact offices refer all underwriting decisions to their overseas registered offices.

The London International Insurance and Reinsurance Market Association (LIRMA) is the non-marine company market's main reinsurance association, providing, *inter alia*, information and research services for its members.

The Institute of London Underwriters (ILU) is the marine and aviation company market's main trade association, providing a market place and various services for its members.

In a joint venture, the two associations merged their policy signing, central accounting and information technology operations and, in early 1994, formed a new company called the London Processing Centre (LPC). Following the merger of the accounting bureaux, the possibility of merging the two underwriting centres, some time in the future, has been mooted.

Many companies transacting reinsurance business in London are also members of the Association of British Insurers (ABI), a trade association for insurance companies.

The number of active reinsurance companies operating in London has reduced dramatically over recent years, and the company market, like Lloyd's, also faces the challenge of electronic networking, in particular the challenge of the electronic placing slip.

The Continent of Europe

There is a vast amount of reinsurance capacity available from the large number of insurance and reinsurance companies operating on the Continent.

In Germany the market is dominated by the largest reinsurance company in the world, the Munich Re. The Cologne Re, Hannover Re & Eisen & Stahl and Gerling Globale Re rank among the top 10 in the world league table of reinsurance companies, based on 1994 net written premium income figures compiled by Standard and Poor.

In Switzerland the market is dominated by the Swiss Re, which ranks second in the world and writes approximately 65 per cent of Switzerland's reinsurance premiums. The Winterthur Group is based there too.

France, Italy and Holland also provide substantial amounts of international capacity through companies such as Scor SA Group, Generali and NRG.

Many continental companies, particularly in Germany, have developed their reinsurance accounts through strong domestic insurance portfolios. Some of the direct accounts were built up through links with particular sections of industry and commerce, e.g. trade unions and trade associations. Companies based in countries such as Switzerland, with a relatively small domestic market, developed with the help of a widely spread international network of offices.

Many major continental companies have also set up UK registered companies, which accept business in the London market.

Reinsurers receive offers of reinsurance direct from cedants and from domestic and international brokers. In addition, risk placement via electronic networks should also be available to continental based underwriters when LIRMA's European market strategy comes to fruition. An increasing number of reinsurers and brokers are members of the Brussels based network, RINET (Reinsurance and Insurance Network).

The United States of America

The United States is mainly a domestic reinsurance market and the largest market of its kind in the world. The high volume of domestic business and the continental spread of risk has encouraged this development, and the amount which is reinsured internationally, especially with Lloyd's and London companies, is substantial.

The comparatively small volume of business which it accepts from outside its boundaries is continuing to grow. Its top two reinsurers, Employers Re and General Re, are among the top 10 largest global reinsurance companies in the world, based on 1994 net written premium income figures.

Insurance legislation is mainly a matter for the individual state, with the Federal government taking a role in broader constitutional matters. Reinsurance operations can be divided into admitted and non-admitted reinsurers.

Admitted reinsurers are licensed in at least one state and include "alien", or non-US, companies and Lloyd's underwriters. Non-admitted reinsurers are not licensed in any state, but operate subject to compliance with various requirements imposed by the insurance departments within each state.

All states are members of the National Association of Insurance Commissioners (NAIC), which is a forum for discussing aspects of insurance regulations, including securities valuation and accounting practices. Its standards form the basis for many state regulations.

Business throughout the US can be conducted direct with reinsurance professionals, through reciprocal exchanges or through domestic and international brokers. Over the years a number of American brokers have developed into large international organisations, mainly through company mergers and acquisitions.

The two main associations representing the American reinsurance market are BRMA (Brokers & Reinsurers Market Association), and RAA (Reinsurance Association of America). BRMA is made up of leading US reinsurance brokers and broker orientated reinsurers, and the RAA represents all the major US reinsurance companies.

The Far East

The main insurance centres in the Far East are situated in Japan and Hong Kong and, although their international reinsurance markets are still relatively small, they are considered to have considerable growth potential.

Japan is one of the most highly regulated insurance markets in the world and all its domestic insurers accept both insurance and reinsurance business. Quota shares of marketwide pools and reciprocal exchanges of business have ensured a well-spread domestic account for insurers. Based on net written premium income in 1994, the Tokio Marine and Fire, Toa Fire & Marine and Yasuda Fire & Marine are three of its top reinsurance writers, the Tokio and Toa being among the top 15 largest reinsurance companies in the world. There are only two professional reinsurance companies, the Toa and Japan Earthquake Re, the latter accepting only domestic earthquake business.

It was through reciprocal exchanges on their proportional treaty business that Japan first entered the international markets. Non-reciprocal business, particularly catastrophe excess of loss protection, is now freely placed and although there is considerable reinsurance capacity in Tokyo, international reinsurance has not proved to be particularly attractive to Japanese companies.

Reinsurance brokers feature heavily in servicing the Japanese market. The main market association to which all Japanese property/casualty insurance companies belong is the Marine and Fire Insurance Association of Japan.

Hong Kong has established itself as a regional insurance centre for the Asia Pacific Rim and in 1993 there were 224 authorised insurers. There are approximately 10 reinsurance companies based in Hong Kong, which have traditionally serviced northern Asia, China, Korea, Taiwan, the Philippines and Thailand. However, there is uncertainty over the outcome of the 1997 handover of this British colony to China and whether it will continue to expand at its current rate, and hold its position as the major insurance centre in the region.

Offshore markets

A large, and growing number of governments around the world have set up international financial centres or "havens", with the purpose of encouraging, through tax incentives and other financial benefits, captive insurance companies and reinsurance operations into their country.

A captive insurance company is owned by a company, or companies, not primarily engaged in the business of insurance, and all, or a major portion of the risks accepted by the captive relate to the risks of its parent and affiliated companies.

The rapid growth of the captive insurance industry is relatively recent and in 1996 there were approximately 3,600 captives worldwide. The rise in popularity of establishing captives in offshore domiciles can be attributable to the less restrictive insurance regulations, freedom from exchange control, and the absence or low rates of taxation which apply.

The major offshore centres are situated in:

- Bermuda
- The Cayman Islands
- Guernsey
- Isle of Man.

Bermuda is the largest of the offshore markets, housing over 1200 captives. It is heavily supported by the US and it is estimated that two-thirds of all US foreign reinsurance flows through the island.

The island has also become a major reinsurance market and has attracted a number of highly capitalised reinsurance companies with high levels of international reinsurance capacity.

The 1994 net premium income written by international insurance and reinsurance companies was just over $18.8 billion. The Bermuda based Centre Re is included in Standard and Poor's top 30 reinsurers in the world.

Other financial centres, which may be included in the ever-lengthening list of offshore domiciles, are situated in:

- Dublin
- Luxembourg.

LONDON COMPANY OFFICES

No one can mistake the "buzz" and air of expectancy that pervades a London underwriting office at renewal season. Brokers' offices are also hectic places to work in at that time, as placing brokers and technicians prepare for a busy day of risk negotiations and placement.

A typical structure of a London reinsurance company and a London broker's organisation, and the roles played by the various individuals, are now considered.

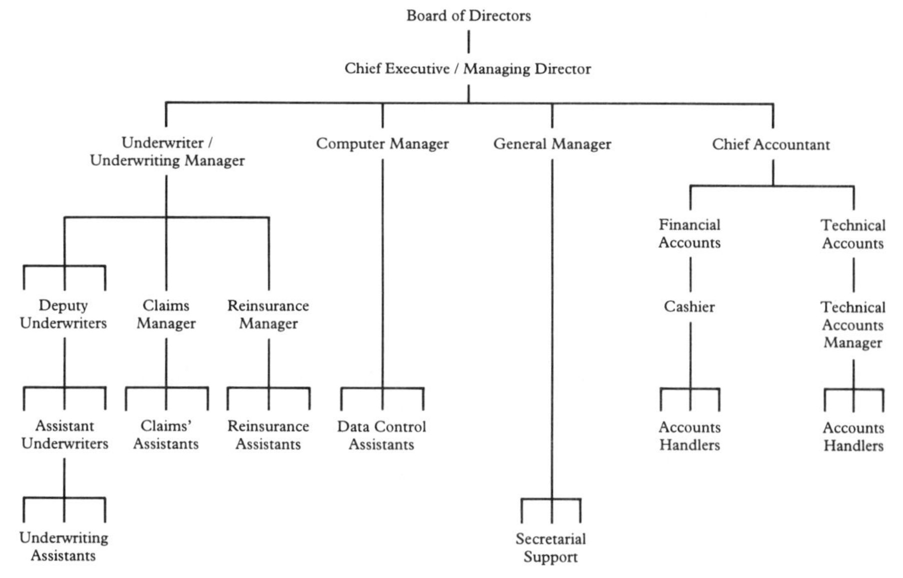

Figure 5: a reinsurance company organisational structure

A reinsurer's office

The underwriting office, or, as it is sometimes referred to, the Underwriting Room, is where underwriters carry out their daily task of accepting or declining offers of business. Although underwriters have an important function to perform, they are only one piece of the reinsurance company's organisational jig-saw.

There is no standard company organisational structure for London companies, but one possible structure for a medium sized reinsurance company is shown in Figure 5.

At the head of this mythical company is the Chief Executive (CEO) who is based in the company's underwriting office in the City, and who reports to the company's board of directors, representing the shareholders.

Reporting direct to the CEO are the underwriting manager, computer manager, general manager and the chief accountant.

The underwriting manager or "the underwriter" is normally responsible for co-ordinating the underwriting, claims and reinsurance functions. In some offices the manager may additionally be involved in a certain amount of underwriting.

The underwriter has a team, or teams, of individuals which underwrite and administer the underwriting sections. Underwriting authority is usually devolved to deputies and assistant underwriters within the team, the degree of authority depending on the experience of the individuals concerned.

Depending on the size of each account, underwriting sections may be split between marine, non-marine property and casualty business, with each section under the control of underwriters who are experts in the respective classes. Marine underwriters usually underwrite their risks in offices in the Institute of London Underwriters' (ILU) building while non-marine underwriters mostly operate out of the LUC.

Within the main classes of business, and again depending on the volume of business underwritten, the facultative and treaty accounts may be split. The treaty account may then be further divided up territorially, e.g. USA and international, with some accounts further subdivided into proportional and non-proportional business.

The size of any underwriting team(s) is dependent on the amount of premium income being generated within the company. In the smaller organisation the underwriting team may consist of one underwriter who considers all types and classes of business, assisted by one deputy and one underwriting assistant.

Underwriting involves the broker sitting down with the underwriter and presenting the placing slip and underwriting information for consideration. If a share of the risk is accepted, the underwriting assistants copy the slip and enter the slip details and underwriting information onto the company's computer using a unique policy number and underwriting codes. These codes facilitate the retrieval and compilation of underwriting statistics.

The claims department is responsible for the agreement or rejection of claims. The department works closely with the underwriters, keeping them informed of new loss advices and the development of large or "event" type losses. Claim technicians ensure each claim advised is correctly input to the company's claim system with the correct claim number and full details of the claim.

Claims handlers are working in a rapidly changing environment. The tradition of brokers advising claims on a "face-to-face" basis with the manual entering and agreement of claims has been largely replaced by electronic loss advice and settlement schemes.

The Electronic Loss Advice & Settlement System (ELASS) is the claims system operated by LIRMA members, and the Claims & Loss Advices Management System (CLAMS) is that operated by ILU members.

The reinsurance manager and assistant(s) are concerned with the administration of the company's outward reinsurances. This may involve the drawing up of a reinsurance programme for the company, co-ordinating broker and direct placements, the compilation and issue of accounts and contract wordings and the collections of claims. The monitoring of non-active security on existing outward protections has become a major task within the reinsurance department.

The computer services department, headed by the computer manager, is the fastest growing section within most reinsurance companies. The section may be referred to as the Data Processing (DP), or the Information Systems (IS), or the Information Technology (IT) department. The various functions carried out by this section depend on the needs of the office and management's attitude to the development of information technology.

IT applications include underwriting information management, accounts processing and retrocession management.

Underwriting information management is concerned with the entry and retrieval of underwriting and claims details, such as territorial aggregation and premium estimates, outstanding loss reserves and event information. Accounts processing provides information for underwriting and statistical purposes and the data acts as a financial entry which becomes part of an outstanding ledger. Retrocession management relates to the collection of information on outwards reinsurance contracts, e.g. event loss accumulations, and the processing of accounting transactions.

IT departments not only interact with internal staff but also with external agencies which provide network and other facilities such as central accounting and claims systems.

The general manager, or administration manager, often has a roving brief within a company, with specific responsibility for personnel and legal and secretarial matters.

The accounting functions are normally split into two sections, often referred to as the Financial and the Technical Accounts departments. The technical department deals with the co-ordination, control and processing activity of premiums and claims. Their objective is to ensure that all monies due to, or from, the company are verified. The in-house technical accounts function has tended to diminish in recent years as reinsurers have come to rely increasingly on external accounting bureaux.

The financial department handles the financial collection and settlement of technical transactions, besides dealing with the traditional accounting function associated with any commercial organisation.

The broker's office

The organisational structure of a London broker depends on the volume and scope of business handled and also to a large extent on whether the broker is "client" focused.

A client focused broker arranges the departments around the needs of the client/reinsured, designating one main contact within the organisation to deal with all the client's reinsurance needs.

An alternative structure is one where the arrangement of departments is determined by class or type of reinsurance, say, non-marine, marine, proportional or excess of loss.

Figure 6 shows the possible structure of a medium-sized broking company which is based on a client focused basis.

Our typical broking company is headed by the Chief Executive, who is supported by operating divisional directors and a finance director.

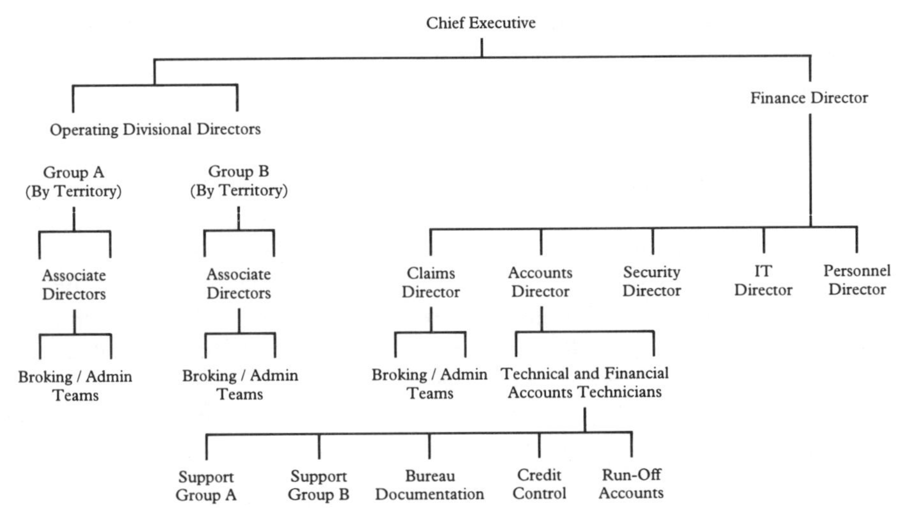

Figure 6: a reinsurance broking company organisational structure

Operating or broking divisional directors' primary task is to generate new business and retain renewal contracts. They have client responsibility, based on the territory of residence, and are supported by associate directors (ADs) and their teams.

Associate directors are designated responsibility for certain clients within the group and operate with a team of producers, placing brokers and administration/technical assistants. They often obtain the initial quotations, setting up meetings between overseas and London clients and lead underwriters. Creating and maintaining good relationships between reinsured/reinsurer is an important part of the job, and a part which becomes increasingly necessary when operating in a hard market.

Producers are the main travellers within the group, visiting existing and potential clients within their group's designated territories.

Once the order is firm and the lead line has been written, the placing and administrative brokers become more involved in the contract placement. Regular meetings are held with the team to discuss placing strategy and various matters such as contract details and placing information.

Initially, the administration staff deal with the preparation of the quotation/placing slip and placing information. They are also involved in overseas placements, contacting reinsurers by way of fax and/or electronic networks. Additionally, they are responsible on a daily basis for monitoring the shares accepted by underwriters. Once the risk is fully placed, the admin staff issue the cover notes and technical documentation, e.g. premium debit notes and wordings.

The London Market placing brokers visit the London based underwriters and offer risks on a "face-to-face" basis. Individual brokers are usually allocated certain underwriters, or sections of the market, say companies or

Lloyd's, to approach. This method of doing business is still prevalent despite the introduction of the electronic placing support system. However, as EPS gains in popularity with both brokers and underwriters, this "face-to-face" method is expected to become less prevalent.

The accounts division is structured in such a way as to support the operating divisions. Take the example of an excess of loss contract, supported by LIRMA underwriters and placed by Group A. The broker in Group A will issue a debit note for the Minimum and Deposit premium (M&D) to the client. Once the premium is received, Support Group A request a Premium Advice Note (PAN) from Group A in respect of LIRMA members shares. The completed PAN is then passed to the bureau documentation section for forwarding to LPC, with the other necessary documentation.

The credit control section mainly deals with the settlement of cash balances due from clients and reinsurers.

Due to the dramatic increase in the number of reinsurers who have ceased underwriting, some brokers have felt the need to establish a separate run-off accounts section. By the very nature of reinsurance business, the processing of premiums and claims from clients and reinsurers who have ceased underwriting, may continue for several years.

The claims department receives loss advices from reinsureds for onward transmission to the appropriate underwriters, for agreement and payment. London claims brokers' long-established method of advising claims on a "face-to-face" basis in the various claims offices around the market has now largely been replaced by the electronic loss advice and settlement systems of ELASS and CLAMS. However, advising claims by post to overseas insurers is still a large part of the claims broker's daily routine.

Security departments within a broking house are involved in the assessment of reinsurers' present and future ability to meet reinsurance claims. Due to the number of companies and syndicates now in run-off, this has become an essential department in every broker's organisation.

As in the reinsurer's office, the functions carried out by the information technology department vary, depending on management's requirements and their attitude to the development of IT. This is an area of heavy investment for most brokers, particularly in the light of present and future electronic claims and risk placement schemes and other international network facilities.

CHAPTER 3

THE LEGAL CONTRACT

"The pound of flesh, which I will demand of him is dearly bought, 'tis mine, and I will have it: If you deny me, fie upon your law!" (Shylock in *The Merchant of Venice*, WILLIAM SHAKESPEARE)

THE LEGAL CONTRACT

Reinsurance generally operates under the same legal principles as insurance, and reinsurance agreements, as with any legally binding contract, must satisfy fundamental criteria to ensure that a valid contract is formed.

In order to decide whether a contract has been entered into, it is necessary to establish that the basic elements of offer, acceptance and an intention to form a legal relationship are present.

A further essential element in establishing a contract is "consideration", which in insurance and reinsurance contracts equates to the premium. This is the missing ingredient in the formation of proportional reinsurance agreements such as quota share and surplus treaties and, therefore, these treaties are termed contracts *for* reinsurance. Whereas other contracts, such as facultative and excess of loss agreements, are termed contracts *of* reinsurance. A contract for reinsurance becomes a contract of reinsurance as each individual cession is ceded to the treaty and premium becomes due.

A valid insurance contract must additionally satisfy the following criteria:

— There must be an insurable interest in the risk.
— The principles of indemnity must be observed.
— The principle of utmost good faith must be observed.

A breach of the principle of utmost good faith or, to give it its Latin name, *uberrimae fidei*, has been the grounds for many a legal battle between contracting parties. The principle of *uberrimae fidei* is probably a more onerous one in reinsurance negotiations than insurance, due to the way in which reinsurance business is transacted. In order that the principle may be satisfied, all material facts relating to the risk must be disclosed to underwriters; it is not a requirement that underwriters must ask the right questions to uncover the facts.

Indeed, silence can amount to misrepresentation, in the sense that non-disclosure of some material fact by one of the parties to the contract will give rise to a remedy for the injured party.

Where a broker is involved in negotiating terms, potential reinsurers must be informed of all material facts which the cedant has disclosed to the broker.

Whether a non-disclosed fact is material or not is often decided by the legal courts.

THE WORDING

It is preferable, though not essential, for both parties to sign a written reinsurance contract. The wording or agreement is the contract document which lays out in full the terms and conditions shown, or expected through common practice, in the offer letter or slip. The signed wording takes precedence over the offer letter or slip and any ambiguity in the wording will be construed, in law, in favour of the cedant.

A movement in recent years to develop standard wordings has received increasing but not universal support. Some reinsureds draw up their own standard agreements, with the details specific to the contract appearing in an attached schedule. Many others rely on the broker to draw up the agreement and so all brokers employ wordings technicians within their organisations.

In the case of London Market placements, the broker will usually draw up the wording and submit it to the cedant and leading underwriter(s), as per the slip. Under "Internal Arrangements" on the slip, it often states, "Wording to be agreed by the Leading Reinsurer only". However, where the leader is not a member of a bureau, this is normally taken by the broker to include the leading LIRMA/ILU member too.

Once the cedant and leaders have agreed the document, it is sent to the relevant bureau for signature on behalf of its members.

The LPC has a wordings department which checks wordings on behalf of its company members. The technician initially checks the wording against the slip details, and, if the leading underwriter has agreed the wording, and there are no queries, signs and stamps it on behalf of all company members.

A signing schedule, listing the name of each company, its reference, LIRMA/ILU code and signed percentage, is prepared by the broker and attached to the wording. LPC attaches to this schedule an Attestation Clause (see Appendix 8), duly stamped. The document is then returned to the broker for safe keeping.

Some following underwriters on a slip may state that they too wish to agree the wording, and in this case the broker will send the draft wording direct to them for signature and return.

Lloyd's operates a similar policy signing service through the Lloyd's Policy Signing Office (LPSO), which agrees wordings on behalf of the Lloyd's underwriters on the slip.

Standard clauses

Despite the diversity of clauses which exists, wordings generally are comprised of clauses, or articles, which cover standard provisions, albeit worded differently. However, with regard to facultative risks, they are unique in that a "slip" policy may be acceptable to both parties. Here, no contract wording is drawn up and instead certain standard clauses are attached to the slip.

A proposed set of clauses for property excess of loss and proportional treaty wordings, as drawn up by LIRMA, is shown in the Appendices 5 and 6 at the back of this book.

The most common clauses which appear in a reinsurance property treaty wording together with a brief description of the provisions included now follow. Any clauses mentioned but not included in the LIRMA wordings are shown in Appendix 7 at the back of this book.

Clauses are dealt with under the following headings:

- Common clauses: Property Proportional and Excess of Loss
- Proportional clauses: Non-accounting clauses; Accounting clauses
- Excess of loss clauses: Non-accounting clauses; Accounting clauses
- Specific clauses.

It should be noted that the name of the clause outlined does not always coincide with that shown in the LIRMA wording.

Common clauses

Property Proportional and Excess of Loss

The clauses which may appear in both proportional and excess of loss wordings are:

Preamble
Scope of Cover
Exclusions
Offset
Inspection of Records
Errors and Omissions
Claims Control and Reporting
Underwriting Policy
Alterations and Amendments
Intermediary
Insolvency
Arbitration.

Preamble: Sets out the names of the two contracting parties.

Scope of Cover: Sets out the type and classes of business covered, subject to exclusions. It is sometimes referred to as the "Operative Clause".

Exclusions: Relates to the standard market exclusion clauses in respect of war and civil war and nuclear energy risks. The article can also contain a third party liability exclusion and any exclusion clauses that are appropriate to the particular contract.

Offset: Gives either party the right to deduct any amounts owed to them by the other party, from the amounts due to them from that party.

Inspection of Records: Gives the reinsurer the right to examine the cedant's books and records.

Errors and Omissions: Enables either party to correct genuine errors or omissions without prejudicing the contract. Although commonly found in excess of loss of contracts, it is not considered desirable as it may lead to a clash with other terms in the contract.

Claims Control and Reporting: Requires the reinsured to give immediate notice of a claim, or potential claim, if it exceeds a certain figure. On non-proportional business a percentage of the excess point is stipulated, and on proportional business a set figure is shown, which is usually the same as the cash loss figure. The reinsurer's right to take control of the claim is also outlined.

Underwriting Policy: Sets out that significant changes in underwriting policy should not be made without prior approval and this condition is precedent to the reinsurer's liability.

Alterations and Amendments: Permits amendments to the contract by way of addenda, which shall be deemed to be an integral part of the agreement.

Intermediary: Sets out the role of the broker, though not a party to the contract, and states that all communication between the parties should be transmitted through the broker's office.

Insolvency: In the event of the reassured becoming insolvent, the amounts payable by the reinsurer shall not be reduced by reason of such insolvency or liquidation.

Arbitration: Covers the agreement of both parties to submit disputes to arbitration, and sets out the rules which will apply. This clause should be included as a separate agreement to ensure its validity in the event of the original contract being declared void *ab initio.*

Proportional clauses

Non-accounting

The additional non-accounting clauses which are common and specific to property proportional treaties include:

Treaty detail
Attachment of cessions
Attachment and termination of treaty.

Treaty detail: Specifies the nature and limits of cession details.

Attachment of cessions: Sets out when the capacity of the treaty comes into effect for individual cessions, and limits each cession to 12 months plus odd time. If relevant, the provision for supplying bordereaux of risks ceded is also included.

Attachment and termination of treaty: Deals with the commencement date of the treaty and notice of cancellation required, before anniversary date, if either party wishes to cancel the treaty. Special cancellation conditions may also be included within this clause, e.g. on insolvency.

Accounting

The main clauses relating to the processing of premiums and claims common to most property proportional treaties are:

Premium
Commission
Accounts
Currency
Premium and Loss Reserves
Premium and Loss Portfolios.

Premium: Deals with the reinsured's entitlement to receive a proportionate share of the premium on each risk ceded. The definition of the original premium, either gross or net, earned or written, is also included.

Commission: This article deals with the rate of commission to be paid to the reinsured and is expressed as a percentage of the gross premium income ceded to the treaty. In the case of a sliding scale commission or profit commission, details of the method of calculation are set out.

Accounts: Lays down the provisions for the rendering of accounts and settlement of balances.

Currency: Where business is ceded to the treaty in more than one currency, settlement may be required separately in each currency. If diverse currencies are to be converted to a single currency then the exchange rate basis for conversion is defined.

Premium and Loss Reserves: Deals with the percentage of unearned premium and outstanding losses retained from the reinsurer, by the reinsured. The clause sets out the timing of the release of reserves, payment due dates, and the permitted alternatives to cash deposits. These alternatives include letters of credit and/or securities and are dealt with in detail later in this chapter.

Premium and Loss Portfolios: Deals with the transfer "in" and "out" of premiums and outstanding losses under the treaty. The transfer out of premiums in effect "cuts off" the treaty with no further liability attaching to reinsurers in respect of losses occurring after the transfer date. The loss portfolio provision may include an option to reassess the outstanding loss amount transferred to ensure an equitable transfer between reinsurers, or may include an option to exclude certain disputed losses from the portfolio transfer. The transfer of the premium and loss portfolios to the next open underwriting year is also outlined in the clause.

Excess of loss clauses

Non-accounting

The non-accounting clauses which are common and specific to non-proportional contracts include:

Period
Limits of Indemnity
Territory
Loss Occurrence (Hours Clause)
Ultimate Net Loss
Net Retained Lines
Expended Expiration
Special Cancellation.

Period: Sets out the commencement and termination of the contract and defines the basis of cover. It may be on (1) policies issued or (2) losses occurring or (3) in respect of liability risks, losses discovered or claims made basis.

Limits of Indemnity: Sets out the extent of the limit and deductible of the contract and the basis on which each is applied to a loss, i.e. on the basis of each and every risk or each loss occurrence.

Territory: Sets out the territorial scope of the cover.

Loss Occurrence (Hours Clause): Defines what constitutes a loss occurrence, setting out the number of hours and geographical limits which apply to certain perils.

Ultimate Net Loss: Defines what constitutes a loss and recoverable expenses. It states that all other reinsurances, except underlying layers, must first be deducted from the loss. The treatment of salvages is also dealt with here.

Net Retained Lines: Sets out that only losses retained net for the reinsured's own account can be included in the ultimate net loss. It also states that the inability of the reinsured to collect other reinsurances, for whatever reason, shall not increase a reinsurer's liability under the contract.

Expended Expiration: States that if the contract expires during a loss period, reinsurers will be liable for the whole of the loss occurrence.

Special Cancellation: Sets out the rights of either party to cancel the contract in certain circumstances, e.g. insolvency or change in ownership.

Accounting

The clauses relating directly to the premium and the claims accounting process, which are included in most excess of loss contracts, are outlined as follows:

Premium
Reinstatement
Currency Conversion
Currency Fluctuation.

Premium: Deals with the amount of deposit and minimum premiums payable and their due dates. Where the premium is adjusted on a rate applied to the premium income base of the contract, or on a burning cost basis, the method of calculation and due date of payment is shown. Definition of the term "premium income" is also usually included in this clause.

Reinstatement: Defines the maximum amount the reinsurer is liable to pay any one loss occurrence, and in all, during the period. The basis of calculating the additional premium required to reinstate the contract limit following a loss is also set out in the clause.

Currency Conversion: Covers the conversion rate of exchange basis to be applied to settlement currencies, other than the currency in which the agreement is written. Where the limit and deductible are shown in two or more currencies the basis of apportionment of losses across the currencies is also shown.

Currency Fluctuation: Refers to the situation where the currency of the contract is different to the loss settlement currency. The basis of calculating the loss payment due to the reinsured is dealt with in some detail.

Specific clauses

There are some clauses which appear in wordings which are particular to certain classes and territories of business. Liability wordings normally contain a Claims Series Clause, and US wordings usually include an Extra-contractual Obligations Clause.

Claims Series: Restricts an event to all claims from the one common cause involving one original insured and to a product of the same design. It replaces the old Aggregate Extension Clause which covered claims in the aggregate for different products and different causes.

Extra-contractual Obligations: Excludes punitive damage awards unless they are claims related.

A book containing various reinsurance clauses has been published by LIRMA.

Delays by reinsureds and brokers worldwide in producing contract wordings, and by reinsurers in agreeing them, have caused many problems over the years. Indeed, the backlog has become so great that many brokers are seeking agreement to dispense with wordings where contracts are inactive and considered "dead" by both parties.

The following section describes LOCs and other alternatives to cash reserve deposits, included in premium and loss reserve clauses.

ALTERNATIVES TO CASH DEPOSITS

Sometimes, particularly on US business, the wording provides for alternatives to cash deposits in the periodical accounts, in respect of unearned premium and outstanding loss reserves.

The alternatives to depositing cash may include:

- Letters of Credit—LOC
- Outstanding Claims Advance—OCA
- Trusts.

Letters of credit

A letter of credit (LOC) is a guarantee issued by a bank on behalf of a reinsurer, which can be drawn to cover a reinsurer's liabilities under a specified reinsurance agreement. It may relate to outstanding loss reserves or to unearned premium reserves as required under the terms of the reinsurance contract.

LOCs are requested by US cedants who, due to regulation, are not permitted to deduct "alien" reinsurance recoverables from their outstanding losses in their financial accounts. An alien reinsurer is one who is "not admitted", i.e. not licensed to conduct reinsurance in the various US states.

The issue of an LOC is not a cash transaction but merely a pledge by an acceptable bank to guarantee to meet a demand for money. The main conditions which an LOC must meet, to be acceptable to the US authorities, are that it must be:

— Irrevocable—it cannot be terminated without the beneficiary's agreement.
— Renewable automatically if liability still exists, unless notice is given by reinsurers. This condition makes it an "evergreen" LOC.
— Unconditional.
— Clean.

LOCs may be issued against the reinsured's instructions via the London Market Scheme, an LOC procedure which is administered by Citibank.

The London Market Scheme was launched in 1964 and is available to all London Market participants. Under the scheme, a cedant, who may have as many as 40 or 50 companies participating on a single contract, is issued with one LOC. Prior to the scheme, 40 or 50 LOCs were issued by the bank.

When the cedant, or beneficiary, requests an LOC, the LOC application is prepared by the broker and submitted to the reinsurers for agreement and signature, using a standard request form. This form is then passed to the bank who issues the LOC and sends a copy to the beneficiary.

Figure 7 shows the stages in the issue of a new LOC under the scheme.

The process starts at Key 1, which denotes the request for an LOC from the beneficiary, a US insurance company. The various stages are listed in numerical order concluding at Key 10, which denotes the signing and return of the trust agreement to the attorneys, Mendes & Mount.

Mendes & Mount, a firm of New York attorneys who act solely on behalf of the reinsurers (Key 8), prepares the trust agreement and forwards it, along with the original LOC, to the cedant/beneficiary for execution. Mendes & Mount also monitors pending reductions and drawings and reports back to its London clients; if a cedant does not act in accordance with the trust agreement, Mendes & Mount will contact either the US intermediary or cedant directly in order to resolve the situation.

In view of the credit commitment given by a bank, it only grants LOCs when satisfied that the reinsurer is financially sound for the full amount of all LOCs granted. Most banks now require their clients to provide collateral against the LOC amount, and usually a mixture of cash and security deposits are acceptable.

Banks do make a charge to reinsurers for providing this credit facility and pay a rate of interest on cash deposited.

Outstanding claims advance

An outstanding claims advance is an advance of cash made by the reinsurer, sometimes under trust to a third party, to cover outstanding losses on a reinsurance agreement.

If a third party, i.e. a bank, is appointed, the party becomes a trustee of the money and is authorised to release the necessary amounts to the cedant, once proof of loss settlement is produced and it has been agreed by the reinsurer. If no third party is appointed the OCA may be dealt with in the same way as a cash deposit, with the OCA retained and released on a yearly revolving basis, in the periodical accounts.

Trusts

Some reinsurance companies with strong ties and large volumes of business with few reinsureds may choose not to put up LOCs for outstanding liabilities but, instead, to place a variety of assets into a trust fund.

In 1939 the first insurance trust was set up when Lloyd's established the Lloyd's American Trust Fund (LATF). The LATF gives Lloyd's underwriters an "admitted" status for US regulatory purposes and the fund currently amounts to several billion dollars.

Trusts must be established by a single reinsurer for the benefit of a single beneficiary. They can, however, relate to several contracts over a number of underwriting years.

In the US, trusts must be funded with US domestic investments, held in trust in the US with a Federal Reserve member bank and must not be less than 102 per cent of a reinsurer's outstanding liabilities.

Currently the use of trusts has been primarily by large European reinsurers in view of their tendency to write business direct, and to establish strong ties with their cedants. Trusts are, however, becoming increasingly popular, particularly with offshore and captive reinsurers.

REINSURANCE ACCOUNTING

There are two distinct accounting procedures within a reinsurance company:

- — the technical accounting procedure, and
- — the financial accounting procedure.

Although intertwined to produce a final financial position, it is the technical aspect of reinsurance accounting with which this book is concerned.

The technical account, or closing, is an advice detailing the specific financial obligations per risk between the contracting parties. These obligations relate to premiums, claims, commissions and reserves, more generally set out in the contract wording.

A New Letter of Credit

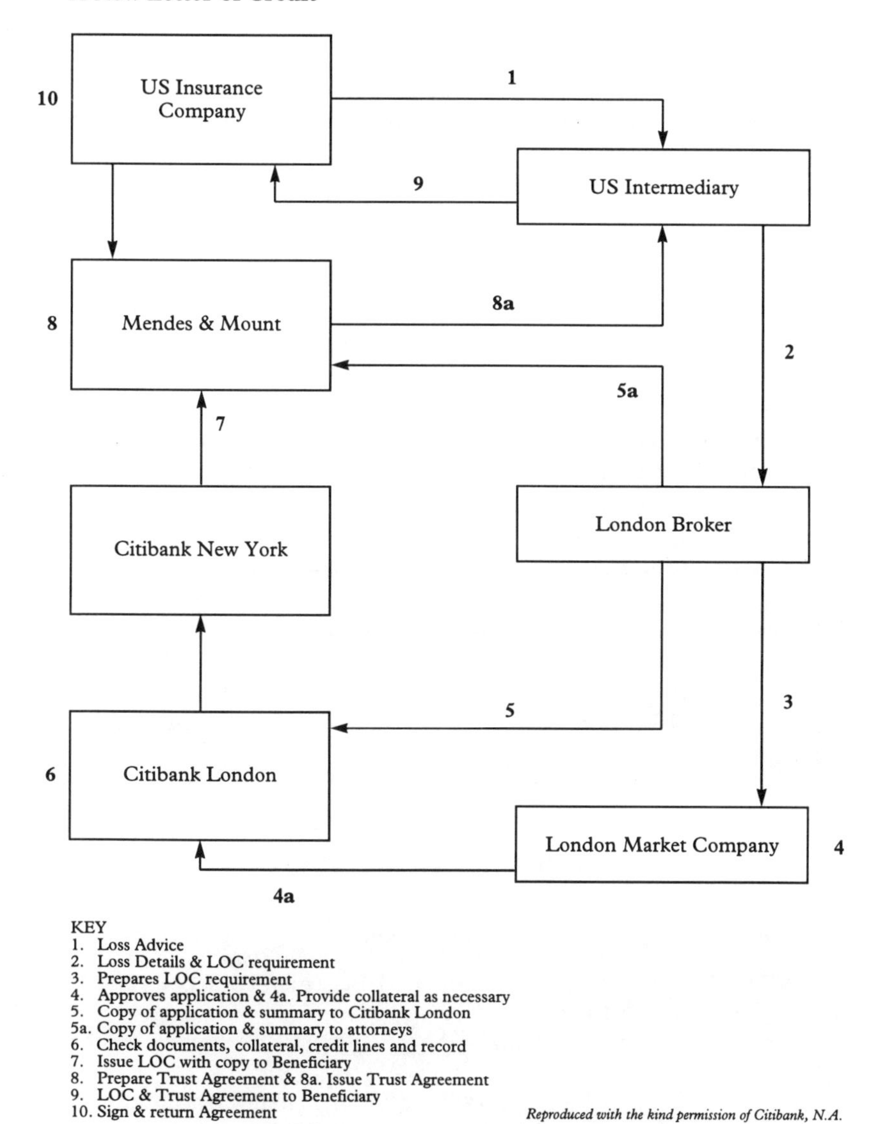

Figure 7: London Market Letter of Credit Scheme

The closing, at each accounting stage, identifies the net amount due to, or from, reinsurers and the brokerage due to the broker.

In the case of proportional treaty business, closings are initially prepared by the reinsured, usually on a quarterly basis, and, if the two parties are dealing direct, are issued to reinsurers. If a broker's services have been used, then the closing is issued to the broker for processing.

From the details supplied, brokers normally generate their own closing for onward transmission to reinsurers, including in the account an entry for brokerage.

Facultative and excess of loss closings are also prepared by the cedant, unless a broker is involved in the placement of the risk. In the latter situation, the broker prepares and issues a debit note to the cedant requesting payment of the premium, and also issues a technical closing to reinsurers advising them of the premium and brokerage due.

Settlement of the closing may be made direct between the contracting parties in "direct" placements, or to the broker in all other cases.

In London, if the services of a central accounting bureau are used for proportional, facultative or excess of loss business, the broker issues the closing documentation to the bureau for processing only after having received the balances due from the reinsured. This situation applies where reinsurers on the slip are also members of the bureau's central settlement scheme, and credit balances to reinsurers are automatically debited from the broker's bank account once the closing has been processed.

Figures 8 and 9 outline the possible flows of accounting information in respect of proportional treaty business and excess of loss business respectively.

In a few cases, an agreement may be made between the contracting parties to settle the account on a direct basis despite the involvement of a broker. Here the broker merely forwards the cedant's original accounts to the reinsurer, with a separate debit note for the brokerage due. The reinsurer then settles each account separately.

ACCOUNTING BUREAUX

In London the main central accounting bodies for reinsurance business are:

- The London Processing Centre—LPC (merged accounting bureaux of LIRMA and ILU).
- The Lloyd's Policy Signing Office—LPSO.

The basic principle behind central accounting is that the accounting bureau acts as a clearing house providing a centralised checking, signing, accounting and settlement service for its member companies.

LPC is an accounting bureau formed through the merger of the previously separate bureaux of LIRMA and the ILU. It carries out all the policy checking and signing activities, all systems development, the operation of all market systems, and all associated central settlement, financial and administration activities on behalf of its LIRMA and ILU members.

Some history on these two associations follows. In January 1991, LIRMA was created by the merging of PSAC (Policy Signing and Accounting Centre)

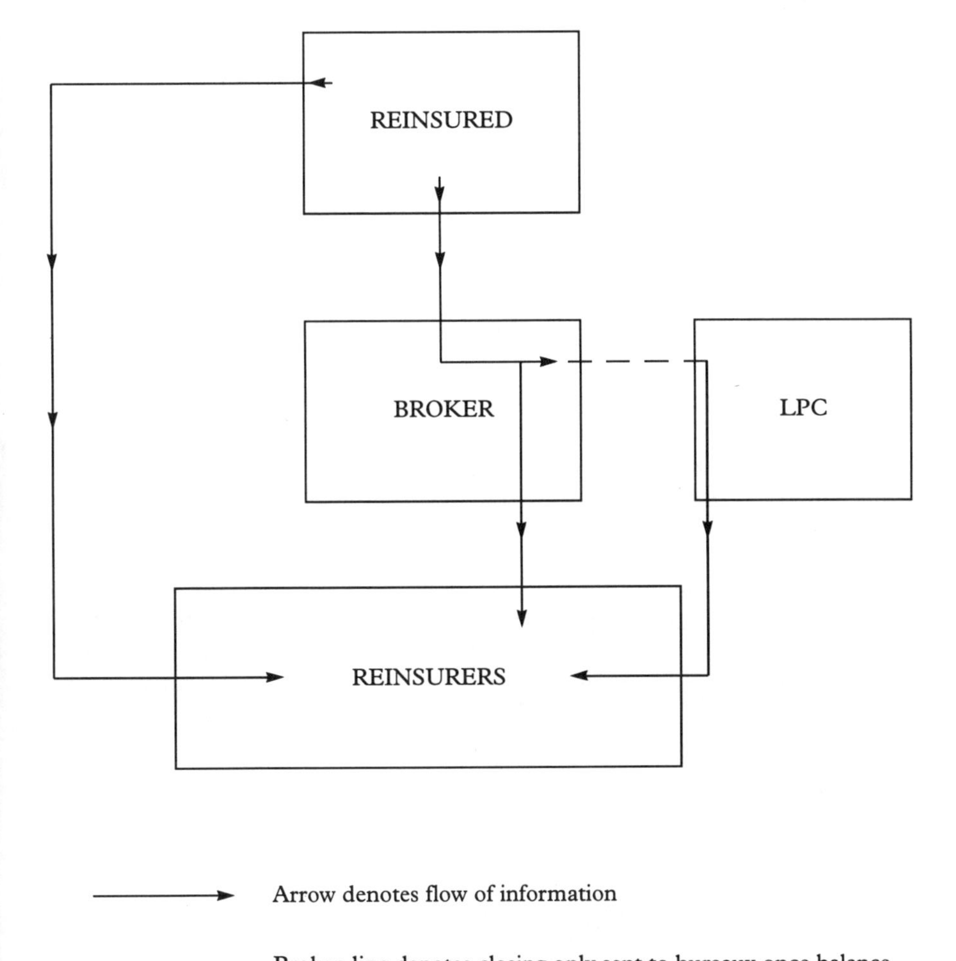

Figure 8: flow of accounting information—proportional treaty closings

and the ROA (Reinsurance Offices Association). PSAC was established in 1977 to provide a cost-effective policy signing and accounting bureau service for its non-marine members. The ROA, on the other hand, was established in 1969 with the aim of encouraging co-operation between its members on technical matters of general interest and its role included representation to the UK government in connection with the transaction of reinsurance, research, development and education.

"LIRMA" now refers solely to the trade association for its member companies, carrying out the role previously played by the ROA, while also becoming more active in the organisation of seminars and special forums. In

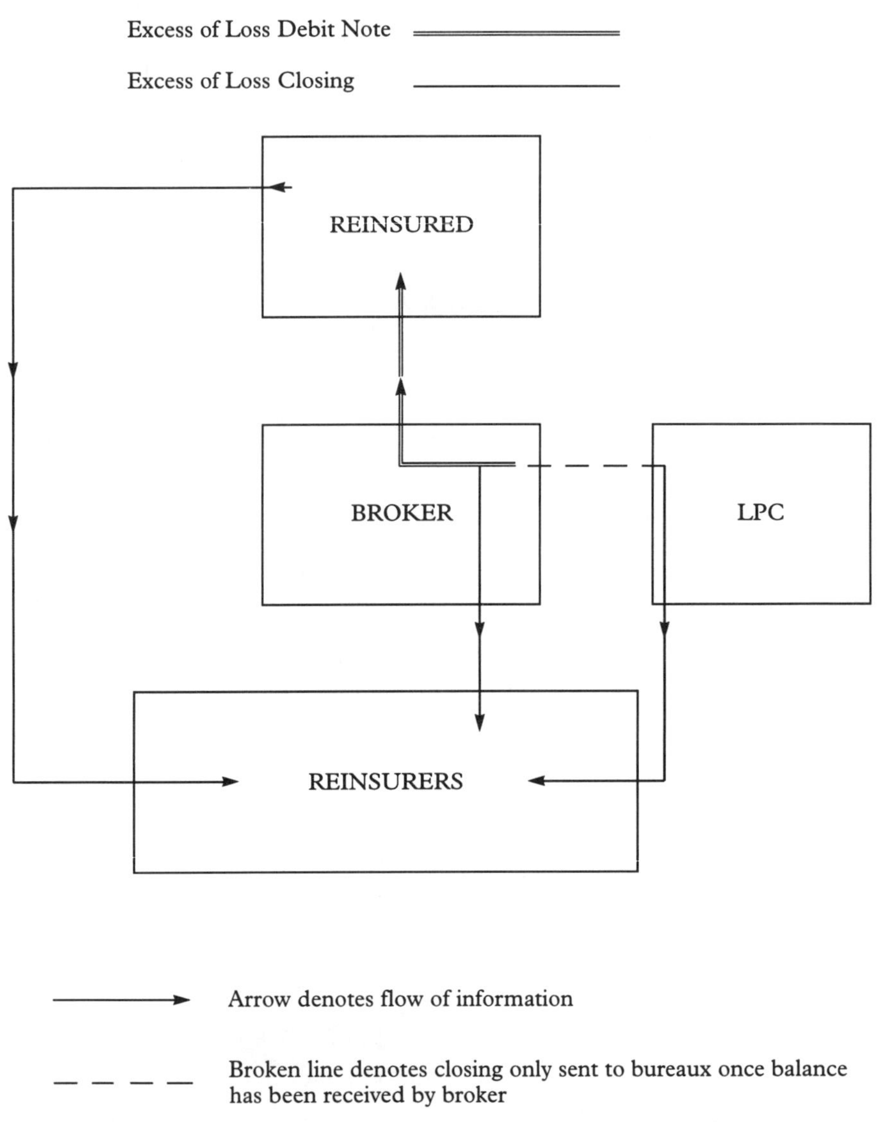

Figure 9: flow of accounting information—excess of loss closings

1994, the association had 97 ordinary members who generated £2.9 billion of premium income.

Associate membership of LIRMA, where processing and settlement services are not supplied, provides over 100 overseas insurance and reinsurance companies with up-to-date information on the London Market. However, in 1996, LIRMA announced a European market strategy, with the intention that full membership, and the use of company market systems, should be open to all European insurers and reinsurers. This would mean that brokers who currently place business direct with Europe could now do so on the same basis as the London Market. Similarly, the company market could deal directly with European brokers who wish to access the London Market electronically.

The ILU membership is made up of companies underwriting a marine, aviation or transport account, and in 1994 its 60 members generated approximately £2 billion of premium income.

Founded in 1884 by marine insurance companies, it has acted as both a trade association and as a central accounting bureau but, since the formation of the LPC, it acts mainly as a trade association providing accommodation and other services required by its members.

ELECTRONIC NETWORKS

Electronic networking in insurance is the communication and access of information by insurance and reinsurance operations and intermediaries through electronic messages.

Corporate networks serve local and remote locations within the same organisation, while the more sophisticated market networks enable the passing of business information electronically between different organisations.

The two main market networks providing services in the field of reinsurance are:

- London Insurance Market Network—LIMNET, and
- Reinsurance and Insurance Network—RINET.

LIMNET

LIMNET was formed in 1987 by the four main associations in the London Market:

— London Insurance and Reinsurance Market Association—LIRMA
— Lloyd's Insurance Brokers' Committee—LIBC
— Corporation of Lloyd's, and
— Institute of London Underwriters—ILU.

LIMNET uses the services provided by IBM's Information Network, and offers electronic data interchange (EDI), electronic mail, interactive services (on-line connections to other network users), and financial and information services.

Despite its name, LIMNET is an international network and participants are not restricted to London operations but must be members of one of the four founding associations. Currently there are over 750 broking and underwriting organisations on the network.

RINET

RINET, the Brussels-based international network "facilitator", was a project initiated in 1986 by Munich Re, Swiss Re and Skandia International, with the objective of establishing a data network for the exchange of information between international reinsurance and insurance business partners.

Its membership is now open to all and in 1995 it had over 200 members with headquarters in more than 30 countries.

RINET also uses IBM's network services and presently offers its members electronic data interchange (EDI), electronic data access and electronic mail services including access to RINET's Information Services.

Joint ventures

Certain joint ventures, or initiatives, concerned with electronic systems and networks have been instigated by organisations within the reinsurance markets in London and elsewhere. The two primary ventures are:

- — the Standards Joint Venture, and
- — the Joint Market Initiative.

The Standards Joint Venture, established in 1992, is a joint venture task force which brings together the world's leading insurance and reinsurance organisations. The consortium is composed of representatives from:

- — LIMNET
- — RINET
- — RAA—Reinsurance Association of America, and
- — BRMA—The Brokers Reinsurance Market Association (USA).

Their aim is to develop common electronic data interchange (EDI) standards and standard messages, following the United Nations EDIFACT (Electronic Data Interchange for Administration, Commerce and Transport) standards.

The fundamental objective of standard EDI messages is to facilitate automatic collaboration between the many independently managed computers in the world insurance industry.

Initially, Joint Venture developed messages are likely to be used within the individual sponsoring communities but, ultimately, these common standards will enable the free flow of information across community boundaries, see Figure 10.

Joint Market Initiatives (JMIs) are a London phenomenon, sponsored by the four LIMNET shareholders, LIRMA, LIBC, Lloyd's and ILU. The first JMI has involved the whole of the London Market in a concerted venture to develop an Electronic Placing Support system (EPS). This system is now in operation and constantly being enhanced to meet the needs of the market users.

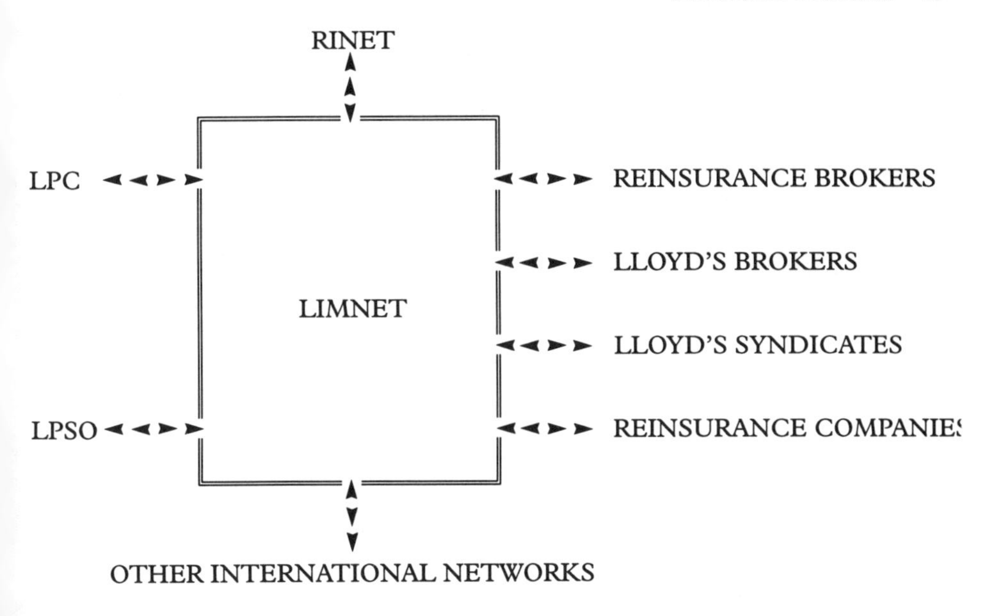

Figure 10: networking through LIMNET

Further JMIs are being developed, for example Electronic Closing and Accounting system (ECA). This initiative deals with the electronic transfer of technical accounting entries, using the standard messages developed by the Standards Joint Venture. Another joint initiative is the Claims JMI group, which is developing a single cross-market claims system with the creation and maintenance of one single central electronic claim file.

CHAPTER 4

THE LONDON MARKET SLIP

"New opinions are always suspected and usually opposed without any other reason but because they are not already common." (JOHN LOCKE, 1632–1704)

THE LONDON MARKET SLIP

In the London Market the offer of business to London underwriters on a "slip" has been a long-standing tradition. The slip sets out the main terms and conditions of the risk and affirms a legal contract between reinsured and reinsurers. It is also the basis for drawing up the contract wording, and confirms the contract between underwriter and broker as regards the payment of brokerage.

In earlier days the size and layout of slips used by brokers differed, depending on common practice within the broking company. Typically, they consisted of a horizontal length of stiff paper, in three equal sections, which when folded became the size of one section.

The amount and detail of the terms and conditions shown were somewhat haphazard, often making underwriters' task of examining the slip terms very time consuming.

As the volume of business handled by underwriters increased, accounting and administrative systems became popular, if not essential. So it was in 1971 that Lloyd's requirement for certain information which was necessary to process documentation led to the introduction of a standard London Market placing slip.

The standard placing slip, in addition to assisting underwriters in identifying the risk terms, facilitated the ease with which accounts could be accurately processed. A clear, well defined set of risk terms is vital to any contract, but particularly so when several brokers and underwriters are separately involved in the offer and acceptance process.

With the onset of word processing, the initial slip has now been replaced by the standard A4 slip.

THE A4 SLIP

The A4 slip follows the layout of the previous standard slip, except it is made up of a number of A4 sized sheets of paper in a book-like form.

The front cover of the slip, Appendix 4, displays predefined areas for the entry of administrative information and risk identification. Also, the broker's unique LPSO number and pseudonym are shown in the top right-hand corner of the cover and, in the lower half of the cover, there are three boxes headed up "for LPSO use", "for ILU use" and "for LIRMA use", and here the policy signing numbers and dates are entered. The policy signing number and date is the reference number allocated by each bureau if involved on that specific risk.

Page 1 of the slip, Appendix 4, shows an administrative data grid with various boxes for completion by the broker, relating to information such as unique market reference, total signed line and gross premium. The example shown refers to a non-treaty slip only and although the treaty page is basically the same, it does not include the extra information boxes at the foot of the page.

Page 2, and subsequent numbered pages of the slip, contain the placing terms and information of the risk, followed by the contracting underwriters' stamps, duly referenced and signed.

SLIP ADMINISTRATION

Leading underwriters have certain administrative tasks to perform on behalf of the following market which include the registration of the slip and setting of the premium terms of trade.

Having entered the line and company stamp on the slip, the terms of trade stamp and a slip registration form are completed and a copy of the slip taken, before the slip is returned to the broker. It is the entering of the terms of trade and the registering of the slip which enable the subsequent monitoring of premium payments.

Terms of Trade

Terms of Trade (TOT) refers to the period of credit permitted by reinsurers for payment of the first and subsequent premiums.

Each underwriter possesses a TOT stamp and a list of reasonable credit terms for each type and territory of business. An example of a LIRMA member's TOT stamp is shown in Figure 11.

The TOT stamp must be placed clearly in the body of the slip at the end of the placing details, with the company's LIRMA button stamp alongside. A button stamp, Figure 12, shows the name of the company which indicates to the bureau which member has initially agreed or set the terms of trade.

LIRMA	Reg'd	Sett Due Date	Def'd	
	/	01 : 04 : 92	+60	+ 120 adj

Figure 11: LIRMA terms of trade stamp

If this procedure is not completed by the first bureau member company on the slip, then the next company on the slip may enter the terms.

The underwriter ticks the box headed "Reg'd" to indicate that a slip registration form has been completed and enters the settlement due date in the "Sett Due Date" box. If any deferred premiums are due, say each subsequent three months, then the number of days credit per instalment should be entered in the final "Def'd" box.

In respect of an excess of loss contract with a premium adjustment feature, the number of days to settle, after the expiry of the contract, should be entered to the right of the stamp.

In Figure 11 the terms of trade apply to an excess of loss contract incepting on 1.1.92, with premiums payable quarterly in advance. The first premium is shown as due for settlement by 1 April 1992 with deferred premiums to be settled 60 days after the due quarterly date. A final premium adjustment is due for settlement 120 days following the expiry date of the contract.

The list of credit terms supplied to companies indicates the maximum credit period which should be permitted. However, the credit period is often negotiated as part of the slip terms and may not always be in line with that recommended.

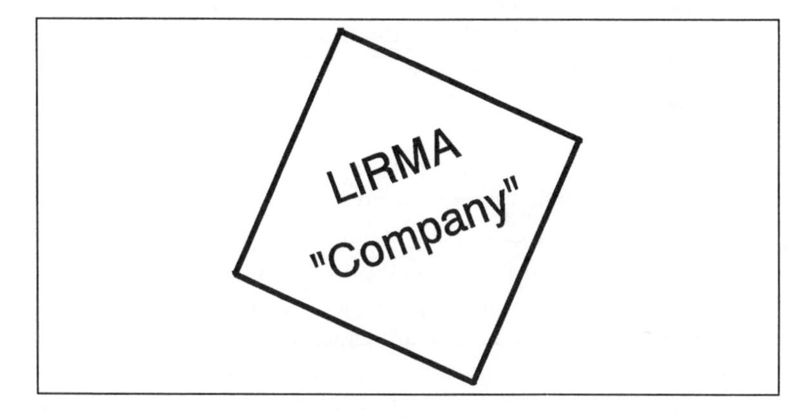

Figure 12: LIRMA company button stamp

SLIP REGISTRATION

The London Market company

Slip registration is the process by which the broker's placing slip is registered on a bureau's records at the initial stage of the placement. Through this system the premium payment performance of brokers can be monitored and late payers highlighted. When the premium advice is finally received, the bureau provides each company member with a report by broker, listing the percentage of premiums paid on time and at various degrees of lateness.

It is the completed slip registration form, Figure 13, which enables the bureau to register the slip. At the time of risk placement the broker produces the partly completed form, in triplicate, for further completion by the lead underwriter, who then forwards a copy of the form to the relevant bureau.

The slip registration form is divided up into four main sections. The first is completed by the placing broker indicating unique information for identification of the risk.

The second section must be completed by the LIRMA/ILU underwriter and contains the company's identification number and reference together with the settlement due date as shown on the TOT stamp on the placing slip.

The third section is for use by LPC only and the fourth section is for use by Lloyd's underwriters should they wish to take part in the slip registration scheme. Any subsequent amendments to or cancellation of the risk should also be recorded on a slip registration form.

With regard to amendments, when the broker and leader agree to an amendment, for example a change in the TOT, the slip should be altered and initialled by the underwriter and the broker should supply a new slip registration form duly completed. The amendment box in the top right-hand corner should be ticked.

The procedure is the same for cancellation of a slip from inception, except the cancellation box in the top right-hand corner should be ticked.

In all cases the company completing the form must enter its button stamp in the top left hand corner of the form.

Slip participation

LIRMA companies on the slip, other than the registering company, may register their participation with LPC by entering the slip registration number electronically over the LIMNET system. If, at the entry stage, the slip has not been registered with LPC, the system continues to search for the quoted slip registration number for up to 30 days. If, after 30 days, the slip registration number is still not on the system, the slip participation entry will be rejected. Underwriters may view their rejected entries on a rejection listing.

Figure 14 summarises the slip administration tasks for leader and following markets.

SLIP REGISTRATION FORM

For the London Market

AMENDMENT

CANCELLATION

TO BE COMPLETED BY BROKER

1 BROKER NO

2 PSEUDONYM

3 BROKER REFERENCE 1

4 BROKER REFERENCE 2

5 INCEPTION/AGREEMENT START DATE

6 BROKER CONTACT

7 SHORT NAME OF ASSURED/ACCOUNT

INDICATE SLIP TYPE

8 FACULTATIVE XL TREATY

ENDORSEMENT

BINDING AUTHORITY

LINE SLIP MASTER COVER

OFF SLIP

COVER

TREATY SCHEME

9 FDO REQUIRED

TO BE COMPLETED BY UNDERWRITER (ILU/LLOYD'S/PSAC)

10 COMPANY/SYNDICATE IDENTIFICATION

11, 12 COMPANY/SYNDICATE REFERENCE(S)

13 TERMS OF CREDIT yy mm

OR

14 SETTLEMENT DUE DATE dd mm yy

PSAC USE ONLY

15 COMPANY WRITTEN LINE

16 EST. 100% SLIP ORD PREM

17 CURRENCY CODE (ISO)

LLOYD'S USE ONLY

18 INDICATE IF ESTIMATE

19

SLIP ORDER PREMIUM (WHOLE FIGURES)

20 £

21 US$

22 CAN$

SLIP ORDER PREMIUM LIMITS (WHOLE FIGURES)

23

24

25

RELATED SLIP BROKER NO. PSEUD. & REFERENCE(S) (if applicable)

26

27

28

29

ACCOUNTING FREQUENCY

30 MONTHLY

QUARTERLY

HALF YEARLY

ANNUALLY

IRREGULAR

AS KNOWN

IRREGULAR SETTLEMENT DUE DATE(S) dd mm yy

31 32 33

34 35 36

37 38 39

40 41 42

S.R.170

Figure 13: slip registration form

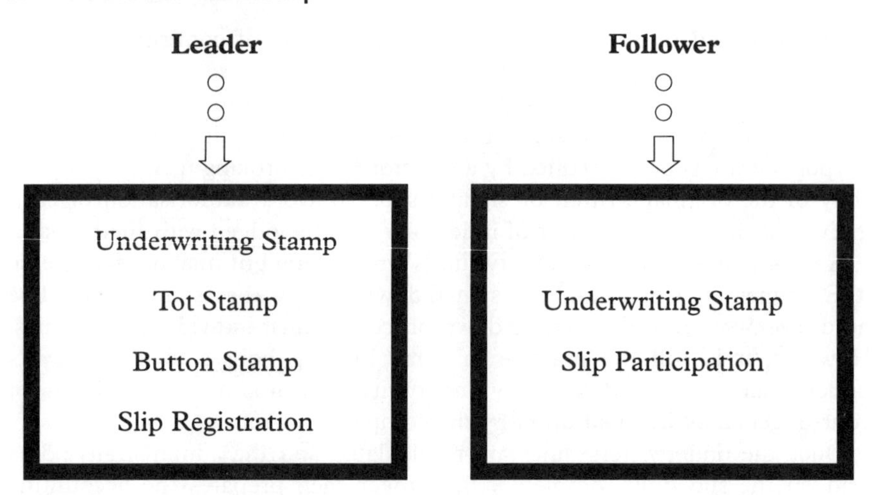

Figure 14: slip administration

Information listings

The registering of underwriters' participation permits the production of various information lists by the bureau for member companies and brokers. The lists include new registrations received, registration amendments and cancellations and registrations overdue.

When the bureau receives the first premium advice from the broker, the TOT date and date on which the advice is received, that is the entry date, are compared. The risk is then automatically taken off the registration list. A breach in the terms of trade will result in the risk appearing on a late listing.

The late listing shows, by broker and types of risk, the percentage of risks settled on time and the percentage settled at various monthly degrees of lateness.

SIGNING DOWN THE SLIP

In many instances brokers aim to place more than their share of the business. It is, therefore, the broker's responsibility to sign down a slip to ensure that the total commitment of the market does not exceed 100 per cent of the cover required. The broker must recalculate each underwriter's line and express it as a percentage share of 100 per cent of the risk, or as a percentage of the broker's order, i.e. their share of the placement. The recalculated lines may be entered by the broker on the original slip or on an off slip.

Off slips are reproductions of the original slip for use in the signing and accounting procedure. In many cases reinsurers on the original slip may be members of different accounting centres and, as each centre requires sight of the slip, signing slips must be produced in lieu of the original slip. Off slips are normally signed by the leading underwriter by way of confirmation of its authenticity. However, with the facility of electronic messages the use of off slips will become a thing of the past in the accounting process.

LPC also accepts a photocopy of the original slip for signing and accounting purposes if it has been certified by a director of the broking firm to be a true copy of the original written or signing slip. To avoid authorisation of each individual slip a general letter of indemnity may be lodged with the bureau.

A broker may reduce an underwriter's written line but may never increase it. Each member's line should be signed down equally, that is, there should be no discrimination in the signing down process against individual companies. However, it is still the practice in some broking houses to sign Lloyd's underwriters in full and company underwriters down and this practice is, of course, generally frowned upon by the company market.

Once the underwriters' lines are recalculated and the administrative data grid on the slip duly completed, the broker then prepares the accounting documentation.

THE ELECTRONIC PLACING SUPPORT SYSTEM

In March 1992, after two years of cross-market commitment, through a joint market initiative under LIMNET, the electronic placing support (EPS) system was launched. This is esentially an electronic analogue of the traditional process of risk placement, whereby a summary of a risk is transmitted to underwriters selected by the broker(s). An electronic dialogue then ensues and the underwriters may signify their declining or acceptance of the risk, perhaps subject to certain conditions. At the successful conclusion of the dialogue a contract is electronically formed.

EPS is a window based application and to enter the system the company underwriter must first establish a link between his/her PC and the LPC computer. When the EPS icon is selected from the LPC User Systems window, the main EPS system is made available to the user and the initial Welcome window is displayed.

Through a system of menus the underwriter can select a risk to view, using the specific Unique Market Reference if known or, alternatively, by using specific selection criteria. Once a risk package has been selected, the View Windows, for "information–only" screens, and Action Windows, for response screens, are available and the various options within these main windows are then displayed.

Making a response

The broker invitation window is always displayed when the underwriter has decided to make a response to the risk on offer. This window shows, *inter alia*, what role (leader or follower) and percentage minimum and maximum line are on offer. There are three main types of response available to the underwriter:

Write a Line
Negotiate
Decline the Line.

When a conditional written line response is made, a Broker Present button is available if the broker is with the underwriter and willing to accept the condition. If an unconditional line is accepted, it is automatically accepted by the broker.

The final window in this sequence allows the underwriter to check a summary of the response and, by clicking the "OK" button, the response is confirmed to the broker.

By 1996 the volume of business using EPS was still stubbornly slow and a series of targets to provide the basic framework for the progressive implementation of EPS was agreed by the market. However, the system is continually being enhanced and the next major release of EPS is expected to include an electronic Formatted Slip.

TECHNICAL CLOSINGS

A variety of formats has been used for accounting premiums and claims between reinsured, broker and reinsurer. The technical closing or account may be laid out in many different ways, sometimes making it difficult for accounting technicians to interpret the information correctly. Where closings are in a foreign language, this may cause the technician even further problems.

Through the agreement and implementation of a standard reinsurance closing for proportional treaty business, and the standard premium advice note for facultative and excess of loss business, the interpretation of accounts has become easier. However, although used by many London companies, the standard treaty closing has by no means been fully accepted by the international markets.

CENTRAL ACCOUNTING

The London accounting bureaux act as clearing houses, providing a centralised checking, signing, accounting and settlement service for its member companies.

In the market well over 90 per cent of UK registered companies are members of a bureau. Non-bureau accounting within London is largely limited to those reinsurers dealing either direct with reinsureds and/or with brokers operating outside the London market system.

The introduction of central accounting schemes has helped to bring about the standardisation of accounting procedures and documentation, such as the standard premium advice note (PAN).

Before the schemes were initiated, companies and brokers were involved in a far greater amount of paperwork and needed to maintain higher staffing levels in order to process documentation.

As regards the settlement of balances, the bureaux operate on a weekly settlement basis, which replaces the previous monthly settlement basis. Monies due to the broker, or reinsurer, are automatically settled by the bureau through a direct debit on the broker's, or reinsurer's, bank account.

Brokers must make their own arrangements with reinsureds for the collection or settlement of monies due.

POLICY SIGNING AND ACCOUNTING

The policy signing and accounting, or separation, process as carried out by London bureaux is split into three types of entry, Stage 1, Stage 2, and the S & A Stage.

Stage 1, or accounting entries, relates to the processing of accounting information. The slip and a completed London premium advice note (PAN), Figure 15, is processed and the slip is dated and numbered.

Stage 2, or signing entries, deals with the signing of the policy or wording.

S & A, or signing and accounting entries, refers to completion of Stages 1 and 2 in one operation.

The PAN

The PAN is a standard accounting document for advising premiums, additional premiums, and return premiums to the various London bureaux. It may also be used as an FDO closing, that is, For Declaration Only purposes.

An FDO is not an accounting advice, but a way of advising reinsurers that the placement of the risk is complete, and of providing them with their final signed lines.

On proportional treaty business the PAN is used for FDO purposes only and not for advising accounting details.

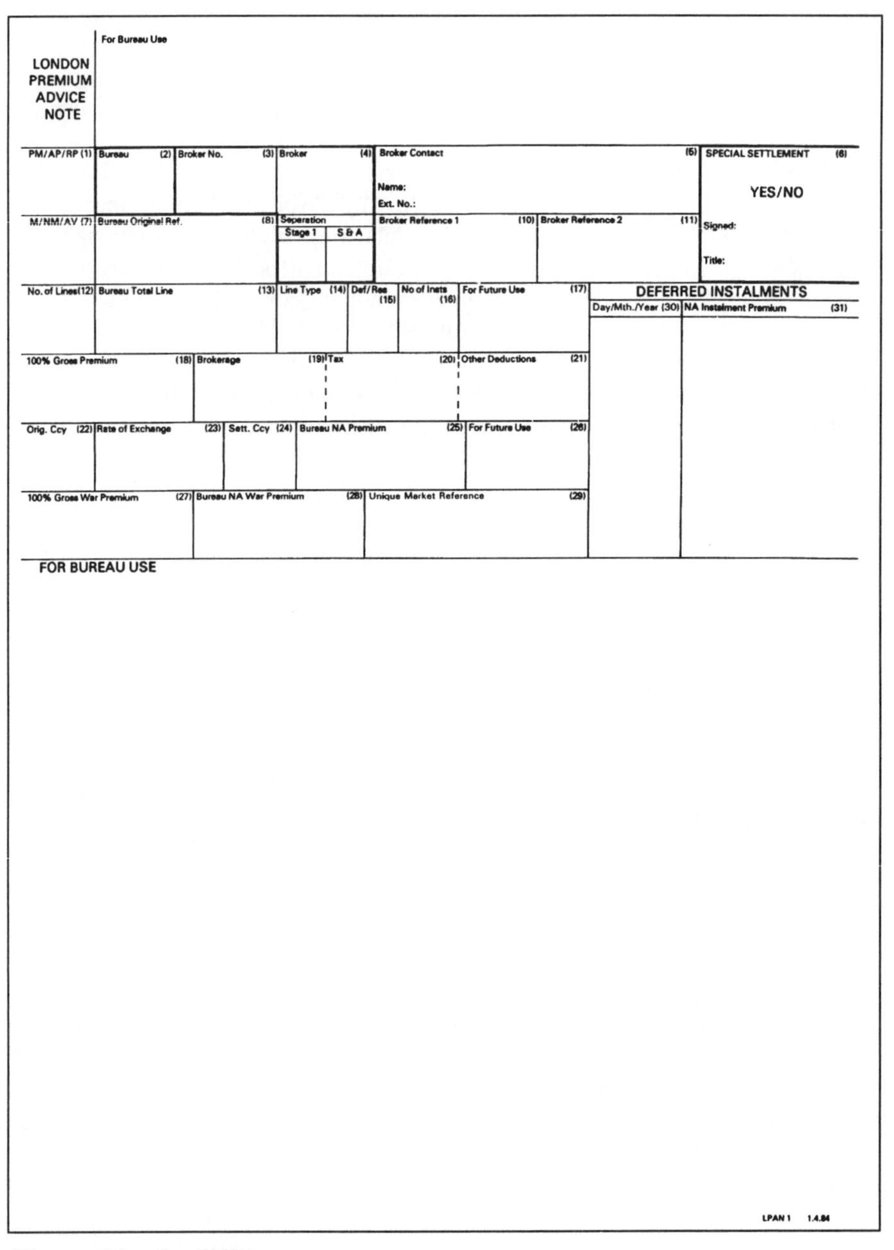

For Bureau Use

LONDON PREMIUM ADVICE NOTE

PM/AP/RP (1)
Bureau (2)
Broker No. (3)
Broker (4)
Broker Contact (5)
Name:
Ext. No.:
SPECIAL SETTLEMENT (6)
YES/NO
Signed:
Title:

M/NM/AV (7)
Bureau Original Ref. (8)
Separation
Stage 1
S & A
Broker Reference 1 (10)
Broker Reference 2 (11)

No. of Lines (12)
Bureau Total Line (13)
Line Type (14)
Def/Res (15)
No of Insts (16)
For Future Use (17)

DEFERRED INSTALMENTS
Day/Mth./Year (30)
NA Instalment Premium (31)

100% Gross Premium (18)
Brokerage (19)
Tax (20)
Other Deductions (21)

Orig. Ccy (22)
Rate of Exchange (23)
Sett. Ccy (24)
Bureau NA Premium (25)
For Future Use (26)

100% Gross War Premium (27)
Bureau NA War Premium (28)
Unique Market Reference (29)

FOR BUREAU USE

LPAN 1 1.4.84

Figure 15: the PAN

Accounting stages at LPC

The three previously mentioned accounting stages, as carried out by LPC, are now explained in more detail.

Stage 1

The bureau receives documents from the various brokers, in a transparent plastic envelope, usually via the City Document Exchange, a private business mail delivery service.

The PANs are sorted into various categories and an entry date and number (EDN) is allocated per document. The slip and PAN are then compared and checked. The slip is checked first for irregularities, such as unequal signings, underwriters' comments, warranties or subjectivities, and the accounting details on the PAN are checked to ensure they are correctly calculated as per the slip details.

The policy registration number is entered and the computer accesses the registration entry previously input from the registration slip form. When matched, the risk is then automatically taken off the registration list. By comparing the TOT date and EDN the timeliness of the premium is monitored and the risk is transferred to a late premium listing if overdue.

Once each entry is processed a master reference number, called the Signing Date and Number (SDN), is allocated by the system.

Completion of the PAN is now considered under two headings:

- Facultative and treaty excess of loss
- Proportional treaty.

Facultative and treaty excess of loss

The PAN is divided into two sections: the first or top half is for completion by the broker and the second or bottom half is for use by the bureau.

The details of all reinsurers and the contract terms of the slip are not entered onto the PAN by the broker but are picked up and entered by the bureau checkers directly from the slip.

The first section

Most of the 31 boxes on the form are self-explanatory, but those which are of particular interest are mentioned below:

Box 6 *Special Settlements.* Since the LPC has operated weekly settlements, the special seven day settlement option has become less significant and, at the end of 1993, the facility was withdrawn completely.

Box 9 *Separation.* This refers to Stages 1 and 2 previously mentioned. If only Stage 1 is being processed, then the broker must tick the Stage 1 box. However, if Stage 1 and Stage 2 are being processed, then the broker must tick the S & A, the signing and accounting box.

Box 13 *Bureau Total Line.* The broker must show here the total LPC percentage line as indicated in the administrative grid on the slip.

Box 18 *100% Gross Premium.* This figure should be the 100 per cent slip order in original currency. The description of the currency will be shown in Box 22.

Box 19 *Brokerage.* The broker must show here the percentage brokerage due.

Box 20 *Tax.* When tax is payable, the broker must complete this box, expressing the tax in percentage form.

Box 21 *Other Deductions.* This box relates to all other types of deductions not previously mentioned, such as fire brigade charges.

Box 22 *Original Currency.* This relates to the original currency as specified on the slip and should be expressed in ISO codes. These codes are standard references which apply to each currency, e.g. the ISO code for United States Dollars = USD.

Box 23 *Rate of Exchange.* This box is completed when the original currency (Box 22) is different from the settlement currency (Box 24). The rate of exchange used for the conversion must be shown in this field. LPC checks that the rate is appropriate.

Box 24 *Settlement Currency.* Relates to the currency in which the transaction will be settled and should always be completed by the broker.

Box 25 *Bureau NA Premium.* This box shows the net absolute premium to, or from, LPC companies in the settlement currency. The net absolute premium is the premium after all deductions shown in Box 19, Box 20 and Box 21.

Box 30 *Deferred/Reserve Account Instalments.* Relates to month/year dates of any cash and deferred instalments. See Deferred Scheme below.

Box 31 *NA Instalment Premium.* Relates to the amount of any cash and instalment premiums due on the dates shown in the adjacent column (Box 30). The instalment is the net absolute premium due and must, when totalled, result in the figure shown in Box 25.

Deferred Scheme

The deferred scheme is the procedure which enables LPC to process items when the premium is to be paid by instalments, instead of as one total amount at inception of the risk.

In this case the broker need submit one PAN only, with Box 30 and 31 showing the amount and settlement dates of any cash and deferred instalments.

The dates of second and subsequent instalments are calculated by adding the number of days, as shown on the TOT stamp under Def'd, to the due date, as shown on the slip.

Each instalment is automatically settled without any further documentation from the broker.

The second section: for bureau use

The bottom half of the PAN is used by the bureau to indicate narrative details, special codings and other information. Narrative details may include reinsured, insured, type of business and brief policy details.

Proportional treaty

Stage 1

On proportional treaty business, the PAN is completed as for an FDO closing, and is submitted with the original slip and a "book slip". The "book slip" will contain future accounting documentation and treaty statements.

When the FDO closing is submitted, the broker only completes Boxes 1 to 5, and 9 to 13. Boxes 1 and 9 should be completed as follows:

Box 1 *PM.AR/RP*—Enter FDO.

Box 9 *Separation*—Tick Stage 1 section.

Stage 1 for proportional treaties also involves the processing of treaty statements, which set out the full accounting details of the treaty. The accounting scheme for proportional treaties is discussed in the following chapter.

Stage 2

The second stage of the process deals with the preparation of the policy document or wording.

The broker submits the wording with the signing slip to the bureau for agreement. A copy of the wording as agreed and signed by the slip leader together with the expiring wording, if required per the slip, must also be included.

The slip leader, that is the first underwriter on the slip, must agree the document before LPC will agree it on behalf of its members.

Checkers compare the terms on the slip to those incorporated in the wording, and ensure that the standard clauses and provisions common for that type of business are included. Any queries and amendments are reconciled with the broker.

Once the document is considered accurate, the wording is signed by LPC on behalf of its members.

The wording must include a signing schedule, listing each member company, its signed line, references, and its LPC code. An attestation clause, see

Appendix 8, is attached to this schedule and the wording is then signed, sealed and numbered. The slip and wording are then returned to the broker.

S & A stage

The signing and accounting stage refers to the processing of Stages 1 and 2 in the one operation.

The broker must submit the slip, PAN, wording or endorsement at the same time. If any query is raised in relation to Stage 1, then all documents are returned unsigned to the broker. If, however, the wording or policy only is found to be incorrect, then the slip will be signed at Stage 1 and the wording will be returned to the broker together with the numbered slip.

Figures 16 and 17 summarise the Stage 1 and the S & A procedures on a facultative risk.

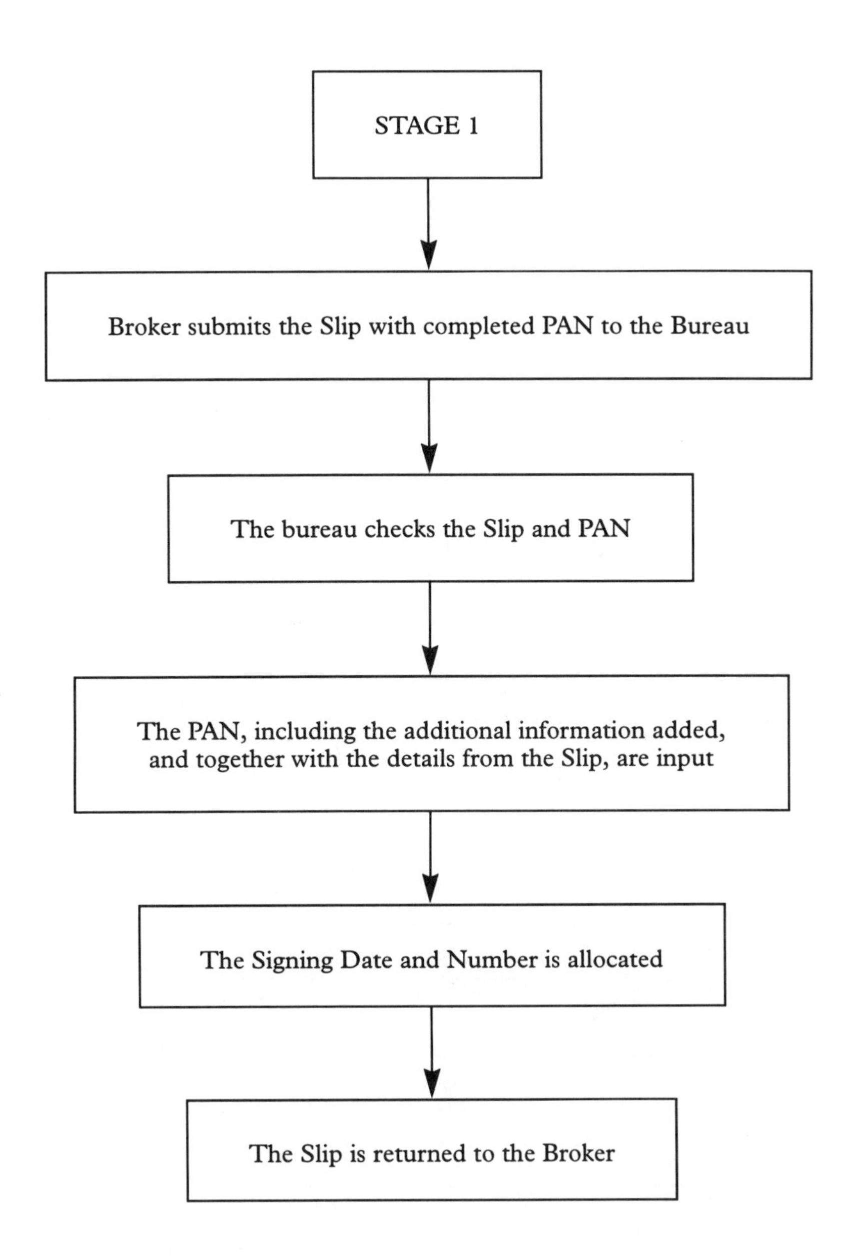

Figure 16: the separation process on a facultative risk

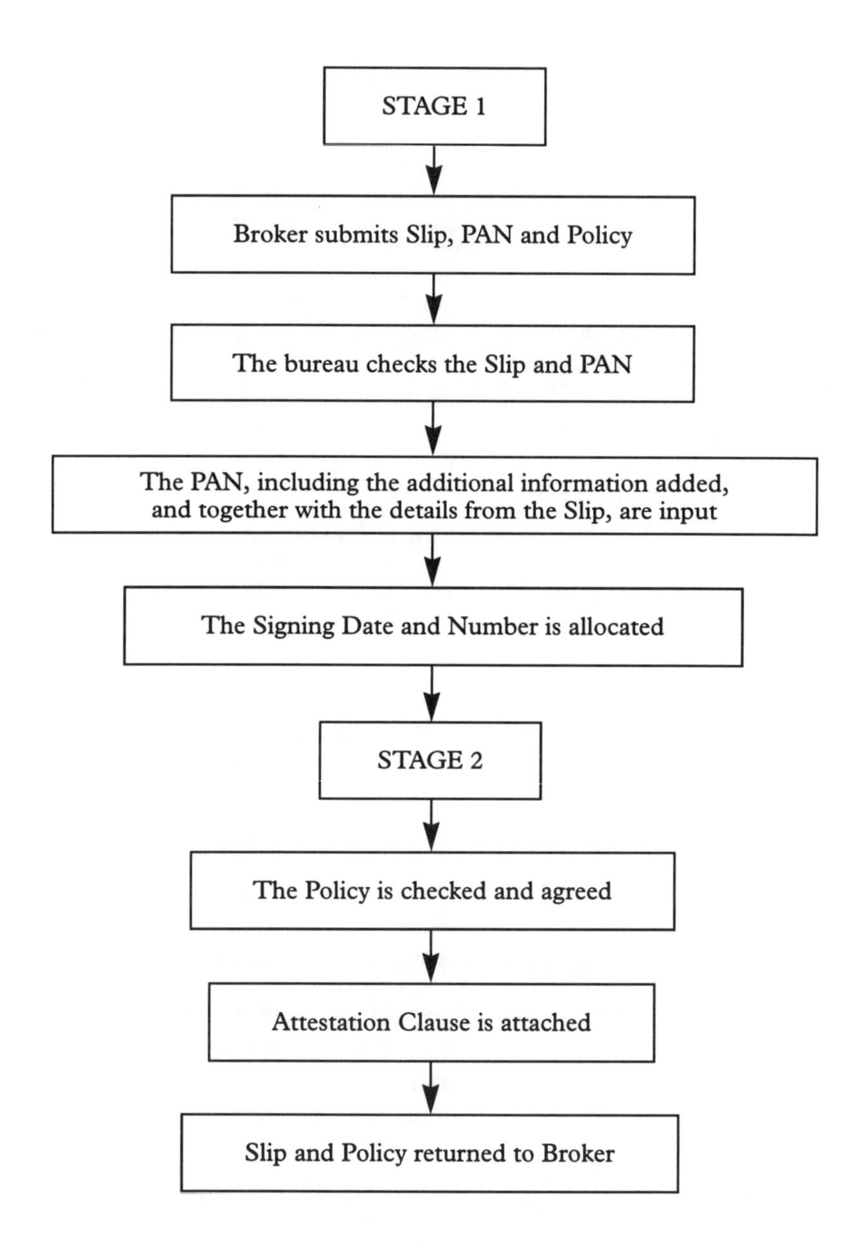

Figure 17: the S & A process on a facultative risk

CHAPTER 5

THE PROPORTIONAL TREATY ACCOUNT

"... and they don't seem to have any rules in particular; at least, if there are, nobody attends to them—and you've no idea how confusing it is all the things being alive; for instance, there's the arch I've got to go through next walking about at the other end of the ground ... " (LEWIS CARROLL, *Alice's Adventures in Wonderland*)

In this chapter we will discuss the technical accounting process relating to proportional treaty reinsurances as adopted in the London Market by reinsurers, brokers and the LPC.

The accounting terms of a proportional treaty state that the reassured shall furnish accounts, usually quarterly, to reinsurers within a defined period of time after the close of each quarter.

An accounts clause may read:

"As soon as possible, but not later than 45 days after the close of each quarter, the Reinsured shall render an account to the Reinsurer of business accounted for during the quarter and split into underwriting years. The account shall be confirmed by the Reinsurer and the balance shall be paid by the debtor party within a further 45 days."

Basically, a quarterly account shows details of the gross premiums ceded less commissions, and claims and claims expenses paid, during the quarter, less any salvages or recoveries. In addition to these entries the cedant includes information on all losses outstanding at the close of the quarter.

It cannot be overstressed how important the prompt preparation and timely submission of accounts is to a reinsurer. Unfortunately, the late submission of proportional accounts has been, and continues to be, a problem. In order that the reinsured can even start to meet its contract commitments, and produce accounts on time, it must have in place an efficient reporting and accounting system.

The accounts must be prepared in accordance with the slip, and as more fully set out in the contract wording. Sometimes the provisions shown on the slip can be quite vague and, as the wording may not be drawn up for some time, maybe years, their practical application and interpretation can be a minefield for accounting technicians.

It has been known for a slip to refer to a provision, such as a profit commission, without any reference as to how it should be calculated. Reliance on the wording, if it exists, to clarify the situation may prove to be unfounded.

Hopefully, this unhappy state of affairs will become a thing of the past as standard slips and wordings become more widely accepted.

PREPARING ACCOUNTS

Once the cedant has prepared the treaty account, or closing, it is forwarded to:

— reinsurers directly participating on the treaty, and/or
— broker(s) who have placed a share of the treaty.

Preparation of an account can be quite involved, and the use of computers has greatly improved the accuracy and speed with which the accounting information is produced.

The format used for rendering accounts varies from one company to another, and this lack of standardisation has caused technicians a number of headaches. However, an attempt to standardise accounting entries, by London Market participants, has led to the development of a Standard Reinsurance Account (SRA).

THE STANDARD REINSURANCE ACCOUNT

The SRA is not in itself a standard treaty account format for presenting a technical account, but a recommended sequence of referenced items which may be quoted in an account. The scope of the items means that the SRA may be utilised for all classes and types of business, although currently it is mainly used for marine and non-marine proportional treaty business.

The SRA may be described as being split into 13 sections. The first section, positions numbered 1 to 21, records details of all parties' particulars, and the following 12 sections, referenced A to L and numbered 001–500, relate to technical and non-technical entries. A summary of Sections A to L is shown in Figure 18.

A full list of the items within the various sections is shown in Figure 23 at the end of this chapter. However, it should be noted that the list of items is continually under review and new items may be added from time to time.

The SRA

Completion of an account using SRA references involves the cedant in only having to enter those items relevant to the submission. However, there are certain items within the first section which must be completed, as they identify the treaty and underwriting year to which the account applies.

Each relevant section must be entered in the account in alphabetical order, and the applicable items within the section entered in numerical order, with the appropriate description alongside.

Details of the premium and commission items in the various sections relating to non-marine proportional treaty business are now considered.

	Section	Reference
A	Cash Account	001–023
B	Premium Breakdown	040–049
C	Deferred Instalment Breakdown	060–068
D	Deferred Account	080–083
E	Premium Reserve Account	090–094
F	Reserve Interest Breakdown	100–103
G	Claims Breakdown	110–114
H	Individual Loss Information	130–148
I	Outstanding Claims Information	160–163
J	War Account	180–181
K	LPSO Requirements	400–499
L	Narrative Information	500

Figure 18: Standard Reinsurance Account—Sections A to L

The claims items will be covered in Chapter 8, which deals with the processing of proportional treaty claims.

(A) Cash Account

Items 001–023

This section shows the actual credit or debit balance to be accounted by reinsurers. In broad terms, items 001 to 008 refer to premiums, item 009 to profit commission, and items 010 to 017 to claims. The final balance of the account is shown in Balance of Cash Account, item 020.

Nett premiums (item 001)

Item 001 relates to the nett premiums due to reinsurers after commissions, taxes and other deductions. Premiums may be accounted on a written basis or on an earned basis.

On a written premium basis, the reinsurers receive the full premium written by the cedant for risks incepting in the reinsurance contract year. On an earned premium basis, the reinsurers receive only that portion of premium earned, that is to say, applicable to the risk run by reinsurers during the contract year.

Earned premiums may be calculated on different bases, including the 24th system, which assumes that all policies accepted commence half way through any given month. Alternatively, and for ease of administration, a set percentage figure, say 40 per cent, of the gross written premium may be retained as the unearned premium amount.

The gross premium and deductions which may make up this entry are shown in Section (B) Premium Breakdown. Nett Premiums item 049, in (B) Premium Breakdown, should be equal to this nett premiums (item 001) entry.

Premium reserve retained/released (items 003/004)

Treaties where premiums are ceded on a written basis may include a provision in the accounts for the cedant to retain part of the gross written premium closed. This reserve means that, in effect, the treaty is accounted for on an earned premium basis.

The purpose of the reserve is twofold:

- It ensures that the cedant suffers no financial impairment if all its original business is cancelled and it had to return a pro rata share of each original premium to its policy holders, and
- It ensures a return of premiums due to the cedant, in the event of reinsurers failing to fulfil their obligations to meet future claims, e.g. in the case of bankruptcy.

The reserve relates to the part of the ceded premium which remains unearned at the end of accounting quarter or year, and is usually calculated at around 40 per cent of the gross written premium. It may be retained each quarter and released 12 months later, or be retained and released on an annual basis.

Premium reserve retained (item 003)

This item relates to the amount to be retained from the premiums closed and is the same, only opposite, as that entered under Premium Reserve Retained, item 091 in Section (E).

Premium reserve released (item 004)

Item 004 refers to the amount retained in a previous account, usually 12 months earlier, and is the same, only opposite, as the amount entered under Premium Reserve Retained, item 092 in Section (E).

Premium portfolio in/out (items 005/006)

The terms of a treaty may call for the cutting off of reinsurers' future liability on unexpired risks at a specified date, usually 12 or 24 months after inception date of the treaty. This cut-off is achieved by transferring out of the treaty a part of the premium which relates to the unexpired period of risks.

As with the unearned premium reserve, the unearned premium portfolio may be calculated at 40 per cent of the gross written premium ceded. If a premium reserve has been retained, then it must be fully released in the account at the same time as the portfolio is transferred out.

Where premiums are accounted on an earned basis, the unearned premium is effectively already in the cedant's possession; therefore, no portfolio transfer out of premium is necessary.

Premium portfolio in (item 005)

Item 005 relates to the unearned premium portfolio transferred into the treaty. It should be effected at the same time as, and be equal to, the portfolio out in the previous year, assuming there is no fundamental change in contract terms, i.e. a reduction in the cession limits or quota share percentage.

Premium portfolio out (item 006)

Item 006 relates to the unearned premium portfolio transferred out of the treaty and should be effected at the same time as, and be equal to, the portfolio in, on the following year. Again assuming no fundamental charges in the renewal terms of the treaty.

Nett reserve interest (item 007)

This entry relates to any interest due on premium and claim reserves retained by the cedant. The breakdown of the entry is shown in Section (F) Reserve Breakdown; Nett Reserve Interest, item 103 within Section (F), should be the same as Nett Reserve Interest, item 007.

Reinsurance costs (item 008)

This item relates to the premium due on a specific reinsurance purchased to protect the treaty. The reinsurance may be purchased by a cedant on behalf of reinsurers, or by reinsurers themselves. The protection is usually effected to cover large losses of a natural catastrophe nature or to "take out" a particular hazardous type of risk from the treaty.

Profit commission (item 009)

This item shows any profit commission (PC) which has been calculated as per the treaty wording.

The PC calculation involves offsetting all outgo entries, such as ceding commission, paid claims, outstanding claims, reinsurers' expenses and any deficit carry forward from a previous profit commission statement, against all income entries, such as gross premium. Portfolio and reserve entries are also included in the formula, if applicable.

A profit commission statement should be attached to the account, setting out how the final commission figure was calculated, and Figure 19 shows how this statement may be presented. Any "original" profit commission paid by the cedant on risks ceded to the treaty should be entered in Section (B) Premium Breakdown, item 047.

Balance of cash account (item 020)

Item 020 is the balance due taking into account all items entered in Section (A) Cash Account, i.e. currently items 001 to 017.

Your share % (item 021)/Your share amount (item 022)/Settlement amount (item 023)

The above items 021 and 022 are the percentage and monetary share amounts respectively, due to reinsurer(s). The settlement amount, item 023, is the nett amount in the settlement currency which is due either to or from the reinsurer(s). The amount is arrived at by dividing Your Share Amount, item 022, where appropriate, by Rate of Exchange, item 16 in the first unlettered section of the form.

(B) Premium Breakdown

Items 040–049

Section (B) shows the breakdown of the entry shown under Section (A) Nett Premium item 001 and sets out the gross premium less all deductions.

Premium (item 040)

Item 040 refers to the gross premium income ceded to the treaty. Premiums may be ceded on a written or earned basis as per slip and treaty wording.

Commission (item 042)

This item shows the amount of commission deducted from the gross premium entered in item 040. A commission is charged by a cedant to cover acquisition costs and overheads incurred on the business ceded and it is normally shown as either a flat percentage rate of the gross premium, or calculated on a sliding scale percentage rate, based on the loss ratio of the treaty.

If the commission is on a sliding scale basis, a provisional rate is used until such time as the final commission rate can be ascertained.

Commission adjustment (item 043)

The entry shown in item 043 relates to any additional commission or refund due, following the adjustment to the provisional commission shown in Commission, item 042, in an earlier account. A statement setting out the final calculations should accompany the account.

NAME OF REINSURED :
TREATY :
PERIOD OF ACCOUNT :
REINSURER :
REFERENCE :
CURRENCY :
SHARE % :

PREMIUMS
PREMIUM PORTFOLIO INCOMING
LOSS PORTFOLIO INCOMING
PREMIUM RESERVE RELEASED
LOSS RESERVE RELEASED
COMMISSION
OVERRIDING COMMISSION
OVERSEAS TAXATION ON PREMIUM
LOSSES PAID
PREMIUM PORTFOLIO OUTGOING
LOSS PORTFOLIO OUTGOING
PREMIUM RESERVE RETAINED
LOSS RESERVE RETAINED
EXPENSES OF MANAGEMENT

BALANCE

Figure 19: profit commission statement

Overriding commission (item 044)

An overriding commission is an extra commission charged to cover the cedant's overheads. When the "overrider" rate is identified separately on the slip, the monetary amount is entered here in this item.

In some cases the overrider is included in the commission rate and will, therefore, be included under item 042. The percentage rate may be calculated on the nett or gross premium, as per the slip.

Premium taxes (item 045)

Where a tax on premiums written is imposed on a cedant, it will pass these taxes on to its proportional reinsurers whenever possible. Any amount of premium tax therefore due from reinsurers is shown on this item.

Fire brigade charges (item 046)

Some countries impose a specific tax on insurers for fire brigade charges (FBC). The amount of this charge, expressed on the slip as a percentage of premium, is passed on to reinsurers and is shown under this item.

Other deductions (item 047)

Any further deductions from premiums not specifically mentioned in the previous items are entered here in item 047. This may include deductions such as "original" profit commissions paid by the cedant. An explanation of the deductions should be given under Section (L) Narrative Information, item 500.

Brokerage (item 048)

This item relates to brokerage due to the placing broker as shown on the slip and as named in the first section under item 4.

(E) Premium Reserve Account

Items 090–094

Section E sets out the premium reserves retained and released in the account, together with the balance of reserves brought forward and carried forward in each account.

An example of how the Premium Reserve Account might operate is shown in Figure 20.

Premium reserve balance B/Fwd (item 090)

Item 090 represents the reserve balance retained by the cedant in the previous account, and which has been brought forward from that account. The entry should be exactly the same as the amount carried forward in Premium Reserve Balance C/Fwd, item 094.

Premium reserve retained (item 091)

The amount in item 091 should be the same, only opposite, as that shown in Section (A) Premium Reserve Retained, item 003.

Premium reserve released (item 092)

The amount in item 092 should be the same, only opposite, as that shown in Section (A) Premium Reserve, item 004.

Premium reserve balance C/Fwd (item 094)

This entry is the balance of items 090, 091 and 092. It is also the amount which is carried forward to the next periodical account in (E) Premium Reserve Account under Premium Reserve Balance B/Fwd, item 090.

Treaty : Quota Share
Accounts : Quarterly
Premium Reserves : Quarterly, at 40% GWPI

Quarterly Accounts 1993 U/W	Balance B/Fwd Item 090	Reserve Retained Item 091	Reserve Released Item 092	Balance C/Fwd Item 094
1st Qtr	0	£ 5,000	0	£ 5,000
2nd Qtr	£ 5,000	£10,000	0	£15,000
3rd Qtr	£15,000	£10,000	0	£25,000
4th Qtr	£25,000	£10,000	0	£35,000
5th Qtr	£35,000	£10,000	£ 5,000	£40,000
6th Qtr	£40,000	£ 7,000	£10,000	£37,000
7th Qtr	£37,000	£ 5,000	£10,000	£32,000
8th Qtr	£32,000	0	£10,000	£22,000
9th Qtr	£22,000	0	£10,000	£12,000
10th Qtr	£12,000	0	£ 7,000	£ 5,000
11th Qtr	£ 5,000	0	£ 5,000	0
12th Qtr	0	0	0	0

Figure 20: Premium Reserve Account

When an unearned premium reserve is set up under a letter of credit, it is termed a UPR. Due to the difficulties in identifying the exact circumstances under which the UPR may be drawn down, it usually remains in place and is adjusted annually.

However, in some instances the recalculated quarterly unearned premium reserves continue to be retained and released in the cash accounts, regardless of the UPR which has been set up. Here, the UPR amount should be shown in (E) Premium Reserve Account with a note that it is covered by a letter of credit.

(F) Reserve Interest Breakdown

Items 100–103

Section (F) shows the breakdown of the amount shown under item 007 in Section (A) Nett Reserve Interest. It includes interest due on premium reserves (Item 100) and claim reserves (item 101), and any tax on interest (Item 102) due.

Nett reserve interest (item 103)

This entry is the balance of interest due on amounts shown against the items 100, 101 and 102. It is equal to Section (A) Cash Account, item 007.

(L) Narrative Information

This section is to enable the cedant to expand upon entries made in the accounts, or to provide any information which may be useful to reinsurers.

ACCOUNTING PROCEDURES

Once the cedant has completed the account, in whatever format, the account may then be issued to reinsurers, a broker(s), or an accounting bureau via a broker.

The technical accounting procedures following receipt of a proportional account, as carried out in the London Market, are now considered from the viewpoint of a:

- reinsurer,
- broker, and
- accounting bureau.

Reinsurer

A reinsurer may receive a technical treaty account either:

— On "paper" from a cedant or broker, or
— Electronically from a cedant, broker or accounting bureau.

On "paper"

Where a company receives a "paper" technical account direct from a cedant or via a broker, the company's procedures for processing that account are usually the same.

Most London brokers, and some companies, use the Standard Reinsurance Account references when conveying the accounting information to reinsurers. However, some still use their own coding system, supplying a list of the item codes with the technical account.

When a reinsurer receives the first technical account, a technical file is set up into which all further accounts will be filed. A copy of the underwriting slip, and perhaps the treaty wording, may also be included in this technical file.

The reinsurer initially checks the account to ensure that its initial participation and underwriting reference is correctly quoted and that its signed line appears correct.

The actual figures in the account are then checked to ensure that the slip provisions, such as currency, commissions, taxes, brokerage, reserves and portfolios, have been correctly entered and that all provisions in the account are in line with the agreed terms of the treaty.

In particular, all premium and loss reserves are checked to ensure that they are properly retained and released.

Also, all major losses, paid and outstanding, are monitored closely and unique "event codes" are allocated. Event codes facilitate the tracking and accumulation of a major loss across all classes and types of business, enabling a full recovery against the reinsurer's own catastrophe protections.

If the reinsurer has purchased a reinsurance protection specific to the treaty, then the premiums due must be shown in the account, or a separate debit note must be issued by the applicable placing broker. Any losses on the treaty that may eventually result in a recovery under the specific reinsurance must also be closely monitored.

The technician, once satisfied with the information received, inputs the account onto the company's computer system, where reference and mathematical checks are performed by the system.

Electronically

A reinsurer may receive an electronic technical account advice or closing in two main ways:

- — direct from cedant or broker via an electronic network, such as LIMNET or RINET, or
- — from an accounting bureau, such as LPC, via LIMNET.

Reinsurers can also receive details of an account direct from a cedant or broker by way of the E-mail facilities available on LIMNET and RINET. However, LIMNET's development of an electronic accounting system, whereby technical accounting details are sent electronically using Standard Reinsurance Account codes, will undoubtedly prove to be a more efficient system.

Reinsurers who are members of RINET may, in addition, receive reinsurance and current account electronic messages from other RINET members using standard EDI messages.

As regards those London reinsurers who are members of an accounting bureau, they can receive technical accounts electronically transferred from the bureau over the LIMNET system. The accounting information goes directly into the reinsurer's computer system where technical, financial and management information records are updated.

Whether the reinsurer receives an electronic treaty account from cedant, broker or bureau, it is common practice for the accounts to be checked by the accounting technicians. In particular, the technicians often need to allocate internal event codes to major losses in order that "event" loss advices may be tracked through the system.

Broker

The broker, as in the case of a reinsurer, can receive accounts for processing either

- — On "paper", or

— Electronically.

In either case, on receiving the account the broker thoroughly checks the details as diligently as a reinsurer, before forwarding it direct to the reinsurers and/or to an accounting bureau.

The broker may raise certain questions at the checking stage, to clarify some details of the account, and a request may be made of the cedant as regards information on known major losses, or possible future losses, following a recent catastrophe event.

Once satisfied that the account is correct, the data is entered onto the broker's computer system. In major broking houses the broker's own computer produced accounts are sent to the appropriate reinsurers, showing entries for their individual share and the brokerage due.

If a cedant does not use the SRA references in the technical account, the broker may "convert" the entries when entering the information onto its computer system. The broker's revised account showing the SRA references is then issued to reinsurers, making the information clearer and easier for reinsurers to check and input onto their computer system.

Once the technical closing has been generated by the broker's system, a copy of the closing together with a covering "confirmation" letter is then issued back to the cedant.

In a few instances a broker may be asked to place reciprocal exchanges of business, although the two contracting parties may still wish to settle all balances direct between themselves. In this case the broker does not enter the accounting entries onto the system, but passes on a copy of the cedant's original account to each reinsurer, together with a debit note for brokerage due.

Most brokers issue financial accounts on a monthly basis to reinsurers, detailing the various contracts and credit or debit balances due for settlement.

If any of the reinsurers on the slip are members of an accounting bureau, the broker must prepare a book slip for submission to the bureau. A book slip is a folder containing the slip and accounting documentation, including a completed Standard Reinsurance Account Treaty Statement, Figures 21 and 21a. Completion of the treaty statement involves the use of the SRA items previously discussed.

Once the bureau has processed the account, the book slip is returned to the broker who must submit it again with all further periodical accounts.

The pending introduction of the electronic closing and accounting (ECA) system means that brokers will close and account to a bureau via electronic data interchange (EDI). This system will eliminate the need for brokers to forward paper PANs and proportional treaty documentation to the applicable accounting bureau.

Accounting bureaux

Currently the accounting bureaux only process proportional treaty business written in the London Market and placed on London brokers' slips although, following LIRMA's European market strategy announcement, this situation may well change in the near future.

The LPC's procedure for processing proportional accounts received from a broker remains, at present, "paper" driven, that is, accounting details and information must be completed on a standard form and sent to the bureau for processing.

The accounting details, once processed by LPC, are then forwarded electronically to its members. However, as mentioned above, the electronic closing and accounting (ECA) system which is currently under development, will permit brokers to close and account to the bureau via electronic data interchange (EDI).

A detailed description of how a "paper" proportional treaty account is processed through LPC now follows.

ACCOUNTING AT LPC

The Standard Reinsurance Account Treaty Statement, referred to hereafter as the treaty statement, is used by LPC for processing proportional treaty and other balance basis accounts; see Figures 21 and 21a. Business on a balance basis relates to accounts where credit and debit entries are balanced against each other to give one final credit or debit entry for settlement.

Quota share, surplus and facultative obligatory treaties, and some lineslips and binding authorities, are included within this scheme.

The treaty statement has a front and reverse side, the front being divided into upper and lower sections.

The upper section is pre-printed and each box referenced as per the referenced items 1 to 21 in the first section of the Standard Reinsurance Account (SRA). The boxes refer to the narrative details applicable to the treaty and reasons for the submission of the statement.

The lower section of the form has been left blank for the broker to enter those accounting SRA items applicable to the account being processed.

The reverse of the form relates to requests for special settlement of the account, that is, settlement of the account outside the normal bureau settlement dates; however, this facility has now been withdrawn by the LPC and the form is in the process of being updated.

The proportional treaty accounting scheme

The bureau receives accounting entries arising from:

- — periodic treaty statements
- — cash losses
- — adjustments or corrections.

1 BUREAU	STANDARD REINSURANCE ACCOUNT TREATY STATEMENT	2 AUDIT CLASS

3 Broker Contact Name Telephone/Extn	4 Broker Number	Broker Pseudonym

5 Our Reference 1	6 Our Reference 2	7 Treaty Number	8 Your Reference
9 Unique Market Reference	10 For Future Use	11 Period of Statement	12 Planned Settlement Date / 13 For Future Use

14 Identification of Treaty	15 Original CCy	16 Rate of Exchange	17 Sett CCy
18 Underwriting Period / 19 ABI Use Only	20 Serial No.	21 For Future Use	

Figure 21: Standard Reinsurance Account Treaty Statement—front of form

	BUREAU	STANDARD REINSURANCE ACCOUNT TREATY STATEMENT	AUDIT CLASS	

22. For Identification Purposes Only

Broker		Our Reference 1	Your Reference	For Bureau Use
Number	Pseudonym			

23. % Signed Line	24. Company Name	25. Company/ Syndicate Code	26. Reference	27. Initial	28. Date	29. LIRMA Company Agreement

For Bureau Use

STS1

Figure 21a: Standard Reinsurance Account Treaty Statement—reverse of form

To initiate the accounting procedure, the broker must submit the slip, a completed London premium advice note (PAN) and a "book slip", to the bureau.

The PAN, see Figure 15 in Chapter 4, is used under the treaty scheme "For Declaration Only" (FDO) purposes and not as an accounting document. By processing the FDO, reinsurers are advised that the risk placement has been completed and are notified of their signed lines.

The book slip is an A4 folder which contains a photocopy of the relevant slip and any endorsements on the left-hand side, and accounting documentation and duplicates of the treaty statements on the right-hand side. It passes back and forward between bureau and broker each time accounts are submitted and processed.

The bureau does not forward to its members any original accounts or bordereaux supplied by the cedant. Any such documentation requested by reinsurers must be sent direct to them by the broker concerned.

The treaty accounting procedure is split into three possible types of entry—Stage 1 or FDO entries, Stage 2 or policy signing and, lastly, the signing and accounting (S & A) entry, a combination of Stage 1 and Stage 2 entries.

Stage 1

In Stage 1 the bureau checks the original slip and confirms that the risk is to be processed as a proportional treaty, i.e. on a balance basis of account. If the original slip is not submitted, then a signing slip, or off slip, is acceptable subject to certain conditions as laid down by LPC.

The FDO closing must be processed before any accounting documentation. The broker may, however, enclose a treaty statement with the FDO and the statement will be dealt with the day after the FDO has been processed.

The broker need only complete a limited number of boxes for FDO purposes—boxes 1 to 5 and 9 to 13. Boxes 1 and 9 should be completed as follows:

Box 1 Enter "FDO"
Box 9 Tick Stage 1 section.

The FDO is examined by the bureau checkers and if all is in order it is processed and a signing date and number are allocated and affixed to the slip and book slip. This is the number which must be quoted on all subsequent entries relating to the treaty.

Treaty accounts

Initially, on receipt of the treaty statement, the bureau ensures that the treaty has been signed at Stage 1 as a proportional treaty. The slip is then checked again for warranties, subjectivities and other instructions. The book slip is checked through for any queries raised with the broker which remains outstanding.

A treaty statement must be completed separately for each year of account and each currency transaction on the treaty, and submitted in duplicate.

Each accounting entry shown in the lower part of the treaty statement must be prefixed with the reference as per the standard reinsurance account, sections A to L. The reference must then be followed by the LPC standard abbreviated descriptions.

Each section should be entered in alphabetical order, with items within the section entered in numerical order. An example of a completed treaty statement, using purely fictitious information, is shown in Figure 22.

Having carried out the initial checks, the bureau undertakes a mathematical check of all amounts on the statement and verifies that the entry items are compatible with the slip conditions. It will also ensure that any reserve accounts are properly processed in line with slip requirements. The original and settlement currency details are compared with those provided for on the slip.

The rate of exchange is also checked and if the rate quoted is outside the tolerance level permitted by the bureau, the checkers will contact the broker to confirm that the rate is that at which the broker was paid.

All entries which have a monetary value must be followed by either a "C", for a credit amount due to the companies, or a "D", for a debit amount due to the companies.

All entries on the treaty statement should be shown for 100 per cent slip order amounts.

Once all details have been input, a signing number and date (SND) is allocated to the treaty statement. The book slip is then returned to the broker.

Production of accounts

LPC produces daily signing advices showing all the transactions signed in the previous day.

Weekly statements of account are produced for members on the Monday following the end of the calendar week. The statement shows all signings processed in the calendar week.

Central settlement

Once the technical account has moved through the business cycle and been agreed, it waits for the releasing entry from the broker before it moves into settlement. The LPC acts as a centralised clearing office for all accounts processed on behalf of its users and has no interest in any of the funds, which are immediately paid to the respective participants. Inpayments to LPC are collected by direct debit originated by the LPC and simultaneous out-payments are made by direct credit to the participant's bank account on the

1 BUREAU	STANDARD REINSURANCE ACCOUNT TREATY STATEMENT	2 AUDIT CLASS

A.N. OTHER REINSURER LIMITED
LIME STREET
LONDON

A.N. OTHER BROKER LIMITED
THE CITY
LONDON

3 Broker Contact Name	B. SMITH
Telephone/Extn	21621/12
4 Broker Number	001
4 Broker Pseudonym	ANO
5 Our Reference 1	870001P21
6 Our Reference 2	
7 Treaty Number	
8 Your Reference	8735219Y
9 Unique Market Reference	213456
10 For Future Use	
11 Period of Statement	3rd QTR 1992
12 Planned Settlement Date	
13 For Future Use	
14 Identification of Treaty	PRESTIGE INSURANCE CO. Fire Quota Share
15 Original CCy	USD
16 Rate of Exchange	
17 Sett CCy	USD
18 Underwriting Period	010187 - 311287
19 ABI Use Only	
20 Serial No.	
21 For Future Use	

(A) CASH ACCOUNT

001	NETT PREMIUM	3,000.00C
010	NETT CLAIMS	1,500.00D
020	BALANCE	1,500.00C
021	YOUR SHARE %	40%
022	YOUR SHARE	600.00C
023	SETT AMOUNT	600.00C

(B) PREMIUM BREAKDOWN

040	PREMIUM	5,172.42C
042	COMMISSION	2,068.97D
048	BROKERAGE	103.45D
049	NETT PREMIUM	3,000.00C

(G) CLAIMS BREAKDOWN

110	PAID CLAIMS	1,500.00D
114	NETT CLAIMS	1,500.00D

(I) OUTSTANDING CLAIMS INFORMATION

162	O/S LOSSES	4,000.00D

ST61

Figure 22: Completed treaty statement

appropriate settlement day. All participants using the LPC are required to utilise central settlement and to agree to direct debiting. The normal settlement basis of accounts is payment within seven working days of producing the weekly statement.

In certain circumstances settlement may occur directly with the member, and not through the LPC Central Settlement scheme. This may arise where claim payments to a reinsured must comply with a court order, or where LPC instigates a correction of an LPC error.

Figure 23: Standard Reinsurance Account

ITEM NO.	DESCRIPTION
1.	Bureau
2.	Audit Class
3.	Broker Contact/Name/Telephone
4.	Broker number/pseudonym
5.	Our Reference 1
6.	Our Reference 2
7.	Treaty Number
8.	Your Reference
9.	Unique Market Reference
10.	For Future Use
11.	Period of Statement
12.	Planned Settlement Date
13.	For Future Use
14.	Identification of Treaty
15.	Original Currency
16.	Rate of Exchange
17.	Settlement Currency
18.	Underwriting Period
19.	ABI Use Only
20.	Serial Number
21.	For Future Use

(A) Cash account

001	Nett Premium
002	Deferred Premiums Released
003	Premium Reserve Retained
004	Premium Reserve Released
005	Premium Portfolio Incoming
006	Premium Portfolio Outgoing
007	Nett Reserve Interest
008	Reinsurance Costs
009	Profit Commission
010	Nett Claims
011	Claim Reserve Retained
012	Claim Reserve Released
013	OCA Retained
014	OCA Released
015	Claim Portfolio Incoming
016	Claim Portfolio Outgoing
017	Reinsurance Recoveries
020	Balance of Cash Account
021	Your Share %
022	Your Share Amount
023	Settlement Amount

(B) Premium breakdown

040	Premium
041	Lay Up Returns
042	Commission
043	Commission Adjustment
044	Overriding Commission
045	Premium Taxes
046	Fire Brigade Charges

047	Other Deductions
048	Brokerage
049	Nett Premium

(C) Deferred instalment breakdown

060	Deferred Instalment Due Date
061	Deferred Instalment Premium
062	Deferred Instalment Commission
063	Deferred Instalment Overriding Commission
064	Deferred Instalment Premium Tax
065	Deferred Instalment Other
066	Deferred Instalment Brokerage
067	Deferred Instalment Premium Reserve Retained
068	Nett Deferred Instalment

(D) Deferred account

080	Deferred Balance Brought Forward
081	Deferred Instalments This Account
082	Deferred Transfer to Cash
083	Deferred Balance Carried Forward

(E) Premium reserve account

090	Premium Reserve Balance Brought Forward
091	Premium Reserve Retained
092	Premium Reserve Released
093	Deferred Premiums Reserve Retained
094	Premium Reserve Balance Carried Forward

(F) Reserve interest breakdown

100	Premium Reserve Interest
101	Claim Reserve/OCA Interest
102	Tax on Interest
103	Nett Reserve Interest

(G) Claims breakdown

110	Paid Claims
111	Paid Refunds
112	Cash Loss
113	Cash Loss Contra Entry
114	Nett Claims

(H) Individual loss information

130	Date of Loss
131	LUNCO Catastrophe Number
132	PCS. Catastrophe Number
133	Name of Loss
134	Nature of Claim
135	Loss Details
136	Claim Reserve Retained
137	Claim Reserve Released
138	OCA Retained
139	OCA Released
140	Claim Portfolio In
141	Claim Portfolio Out
142	Reinsurance Recoveries
143	Claim Reserve/OCA Interest
144	Outstanding Losses
145	Paid Claims
146	Paid Refunds
147	Cash Losses
148	Cash Loss Contra Entry

(I) Outstanding claims information

160	Claim Reserve Balance
161	Balance of OCA
162	Outstanding Losses
163	Adjusted Outstanding Loss Amount

(J) War account

180	War Risks Only (WRO)
181	If no items specified Nil or None advised

(K) LPSO requirements

400–499	This section has been allocated to the LPSO for their internal requirements

(L) Narrative information

500	Unlimited free format section for any items within the account that need clarification

CHAPTER 6

LONDON MARKET CLAIMS

"Sir, I have found you an argument but I am not obliged to find you an understanding." (SAMUEL JOHNSON, 1709–1784)

The primary function of insurance is to spread the losses of the few over the many. In its simplest form a reinsurance company sets up a fund from the premiums it receives and out of this fund all its expenses and claims are met.

The concept of establishing a fund to meet future liabilities is easily grasped—accurately estimating those liabilities is another thing altogether.

The increasing complexity of the society in which we live has played havoc with the accurate determination of future losses. As social attitudes to litigation change and science and technology continue to develop new processes and products, reinsurers have experienced and continue to experience great difficulty in predicting future losses with any degree of certainty.

The accurate reserving of losses is one of the most important and difficult tasks carried out by any insurer and, perhaps even more so, by a reinsurer. The success or failure of any reinsurer relies heavily on how competently the reserving process is carried out.

Premium rates and sound operating decisions are influenced by known and future estimated reserves. Where ultimate settlement costs are correctly estimated, adequate premium rates can be set, an underwriting profit becomes a more likely possibility, and the continued healthy financial situation of a company is therefore secured.

LONDON MARKET CLAIMS

Claims handling in the London Market historically has not portrayed the same amount of "glamour" as risk placing or underwriting. The reasons for this lack of prestige can probably be put down to a general lack of investment, by brokers and companies, in the claims area.

The need for investment in claims processing, particularly for the development of efficient claims systems, eventually came to the fore when London reinsurers' good name for quick, businesslike settlement of claims became questionable. Brokers and underwriters alike could no longer ignore their shortcomings in the claims area.

In 1987 a move was made among the main London Market associations for the creation of an efficient electronic system for the handling of claims. This movement eventually led to the development of the electronic claims systems which have now substantially replaced the traditional methods of claims processing in London.

Traditional systems

The traditional face-to-face method, where brokers personally advised reinsurers of losses and obtained agreement to settle, meant that broking companies needed to employ an army of claims brokers in order to provide a decent service. Visits by brokers, with a stack of claim files to hand, often led to long waits in claims offices.

This system involved the claims broker first showing the claim file to the leader(s) on the contract and obtaining their agreement to settle the claim, before seeking the agreement of the following underwriters on the slip and requesting their settlement of the loss.

Discussions with claims examiners could take a few minutes, or very much longer, depending on the complexity of the claim. The examiner would normally take copies of certain parts of the broker's correspondence file for their records, and update any changes in outstanding loss reserves.

Outstanding losses have been advised in the same manner, but have not formed part of any claims schemes for London non-marine companies. Therefore, possible and outstanding losses have been advised to reinsurers in a rather haphazard way, and often understaffed brokers only updated underwriters when settlement demands by clients had eased.

A first advice with a settlement request was a common enough situation in the market and some cedants only advised brokers of changes in reserves on an annual basis, so adding to the already existing delay problems suffered by reinsurers in the accurate reserving of losses.

As regards claim settlements in London, the majority are made through central settlement schemes run by accounting bureaux. Traditionally, on non-proportional treaty claims, the broker submitted a London Claim Collection Form (LCCF), see Figure 24, to the bureau for processing. The funds were then automatically transferred between the brokers' and reinsurers' bank accounts. However, the LCCF will become obsolete when all applicable claims are processed over the electronic network systems.

On proportional treaty business, where premiums and claims are settled in account on a balance basis, there has not been the same degree of face-to-face contact as only large loss cash requests required reinsurers' previous agreement to settle.

LONDON CLAIM COLLECTION FORM

Bureau/Claim Office Use Only

A	B	C	D	E	F	G
Reserved for Lloyd's Future Use						

1 CLM/REF/REC	2 Bureau	3 Broker Number	Pseudonym	4 Broker Contact Name Telephone/Extn	5 Special Settlement State 'Yes' and Authorize

6 Bureau Original Signing Reference	7 Bureau Original Claim Ref	8 Broker Reference 1	9 Broker Reference 2	10 Pool Scheme	11 Attachments

12 Ccy Code of Claim	13 100% Order Amount	14 Rate of Exchange	15 100% Settlement Amount	16 Bureau Total Line	17 No of Lines

18 Sett Ccy	19 Bureau Settlement Amount	20 100% VAT Amount	21 100% Imported Services Amount	22 Imported Services Narrative

23 Lloyd's Only							24 If Subject to LIRMA SCA State 'Yes'	Slip Leader	25 Date of Loss	
DTI	Audit M	Audit NM	Audit AV	'B' Scheme	US Tax Code	Year of Account			From	To

26 100% Order Highest Estimate Amount	27 100% Order Prev Settled Amount	28 100% Order O/S Claim Amount	29 Date of Loss Narrative

30 Narrative Details

'Insured
Reinsured
Interest
Perils/Conditions
Location/Voyage/Period
Insured Value of Interest
100% S/I/Limits
100% Excess Point
Vessel/Aircraft
Nature of Claim
Nature and Date of Accident
Poss Recovery from
Total Claim Details

31 LIRMA Claim Authority

WARRANTED THAT WE HAVE OBTAINED THE AGREEMENT OF ALL PARTICIPATING LIRMA COMPANIES TO THE SETTLEMENT EXCEPT AS MAY BE VARIED BY THE TERMS OF ANY PRIVATE AGREEMENT OR SLIP CONDITION.

Signature of Brokers Representative

32 Passed by/LIRMA SCA

LCCFI

Figure 24: the LCCF form—front

LONDON

CLAIM

COLLECTION

FORM

Bureau/Claim Office Use Only

33 For Identification Purposes Only

Broker		Broker Reference 1	Broker Reference 2	Bureau Original Signing Reference	Bureau Original Claim Ref
Number	Pseudonym				

34 %Signed Line	35 Company Name	36 Company/ Syndicate Code No	37 Reference	38 Initial	39 Date	40 LIRMA Company Agreement

L1 LCCF1 WITHERBY & COMPANY LIMITED

Figure 24a: the LCCF form—reverse

Those London Market reinsurers who do not have claims offices in London communicate with brokers by post, telephone and fax. Non-bureau companies in London normally agree claims either on a face-to-face basis or by post.

Electronic systems

Claims servicing had to improve if London was to regain its competitive advantage. Much time and energy was therefore spent by the various market participants in developing the various electronic claims advice and settlement systems now in operation. The current systems that have been developed include:

- ELASS—Electronic Loss Advice and Settlement System in the non-marine sector—LIRMA members,
- CLAMS—Claims and Loss Advice Management System in the marine and aviation sector—ILU members, and
- CASS—Claims Agreement and Support System at Lloyd's.

The introduction of these schemes has reduced the queues of claims brokers dramatically in reinsurers' offices. The main advantages for the broker and underwriter have included a reduction in paper work and simultaneous advice of outstanding losses to all members.

Also, as claims can be entered, agreed and passed into settlement on the same day, the speed at which cedants' claims can be paid has improved greatly.

In an effort to streamline all London Market processes, the merging of the ELASS and CLAMS systems is now underway and the target date for delivery of this single "CLASS" system is mid-1997.

The proportional treaty claims system will also be streamlined with the implementation of the Electronic Closing and Accounting system.

The operation of both the proportional treaty claims system and ELASS is covered in detail in the following chapter but, first, we will consider the claims environment and the practice of loss reserving in the London reinsurance market.

THE CLAIMS ENVIRONMENT

A flow of reported claims from various insureds suffering the same loss occurrence, e.g. a storm, is shown in Figure 25 and, although this example may be further developed as the reinsurer continues the onward flow of loss advices to its reinsurers, there are many more participants involved in the claim process than are initially shown here.

These participants include:

- claims examiners
- claims brokers
- loss adjusters
- legal experts
- expert witnesses.

The claims examiner

The claims examiners', or handlers', primary objective is the settlement of claims at an amount equitable to both reinsured and reinsurer. Examiners also have responsibility for the reserving of outstanding losses for known claims, making both objective and subjective reserving decisions depending on the circumstances of the claim.

The examiners of leading reinsurers need to have a good knowledge of how different reinsurance contracts operate and be familiar with the operation of insurance and reinsurance clauses that may be included in a contract.

The claims broker

A broker's legal responsibility to service claims for their client is questionable but, as the client does not generally have easy access to reinsurance underwriters, it is the broker who must provide this service. In any case there is usually a clause within the wording which stipulates that all correspondence between the two parties must go through the intermediary. The claims broker negotiates a settlement with reinsurers on the best possible terms for the client.

The loss adjuster

A loss adjuster is an independent and professionally qualified person who makes judgements on settlement amounts based on established market practices. Reinsurers normally employ loss adjusters to investigate and negotiate contentious or large claims. In the case of hurricanes and other catastrophe type losses, London Market reinsurers usually unite and appoint one firm of loss adjusters to adjust claims in the loss area and to provide summary estimates of potential damage.

The legal experts

Solicitors and barristers are employed where claims progress to litigation and where disputes arise between a reinsured and reinsurer. Before that stage is reached, solicitors may become involved in determining whether there is a viable case, carrying out appropriate investigations into the case and often arranging for an inspection of records to be carried out.

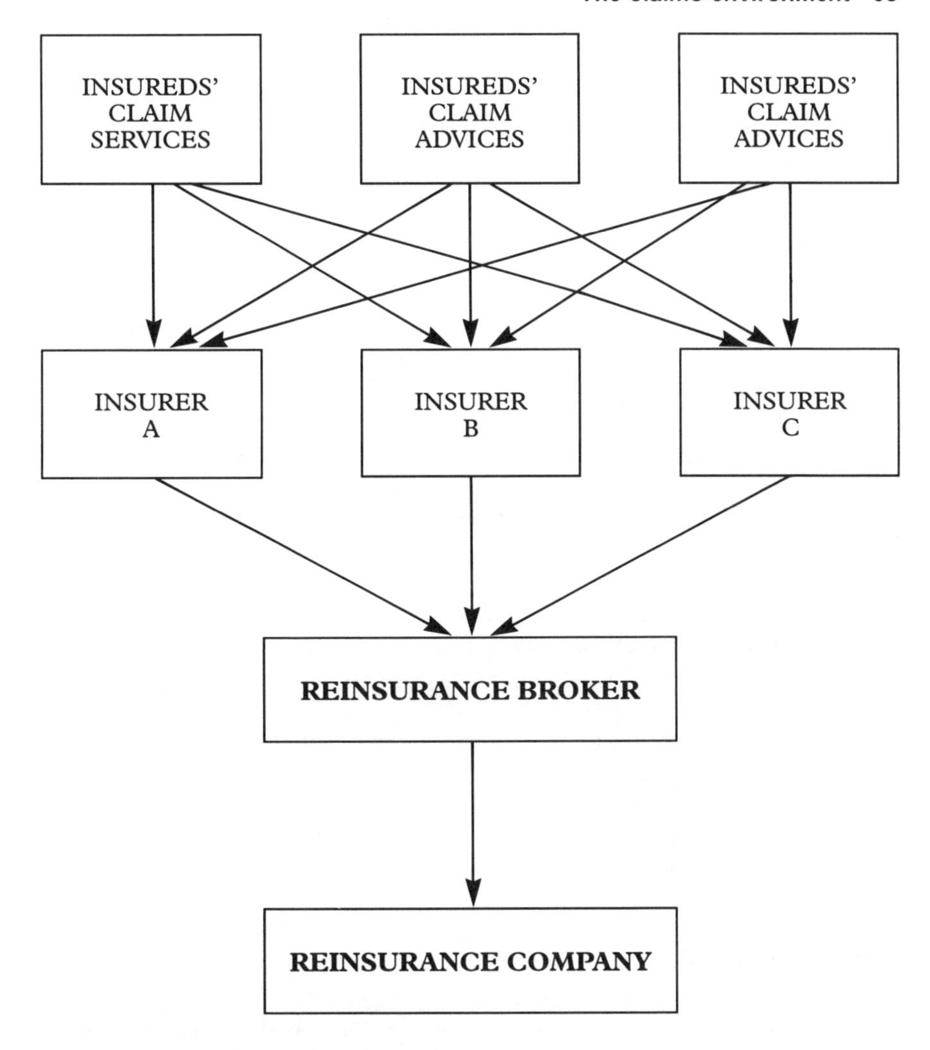

Figure 25: claims report flow chart

The legal professional also may become involved in cases where arbitration is the preferred course of action. Legal costs can form a substantial part of a disputed claims settlement amount and must be taken into account by a reinsurer when contemplating any lawsuit.

The expert witnesses

Expert witnesses are often employed in litigation cases to give their "expert" opinion on a specific aspect of a case. They include:

- — technical experts—including mechanical, electrical and motor engineers

— medical experts—doctors and specialist consultants
— other experts—e.g. reinsurance specialists.

CLAIMS DEPARTMENTS

The reinsurance company

The London company's claims department is normally headed by a claims manager, who is supported by a number of claims examiners or handlers. The claims manager will usually report to the Chief Executive.

The duties of a claims manager differ between companies, but generally they include managing claims staff and getting involved in the company's insurance fund estimations. In addition, much of the manager's time is spent on discussing and negotiating claim settlements with solicitors, on contentious or "problem" claims. Unfortunately, contract disputes between reinsurance companies and their cedants, or reinsurers, seem to be taking up an increasing amount of a manager's time these days.

The claims department receives its daily claims advices either via a broker, or, in the case of a direct placement, from the cedant. A broker may advise reinsurers of a potential claim either by post, in person at the reinsurers' offices, or electronically over the LIMNET system.

On receiving each new claims advice the claims examiner allocates a unique claim number, and this reference, the contract reference, and certain claim details, are then entered onto the company's claim system.

For those "alien" companies accepting USA business, the issue of letters of credit (LOCs) for unearned premiums and outstanding losses is a major part of a claims examiner's year end routine. Although, for some companies, the electronic LOC system "ELECT", discussed in Chapter 8, has helped to lighten the workload.

The degree of authority given to examiners to reserve and settle losses is dependent on their claims experience and the management's philosophy on the agreement of claims.

Claims personnel should also liaise closely with underwriters so that the underwriters can keep abreast of new loss advices and the development of event losses on their portfolios of risks.

The broker's office

The London broker's claims department is headed by a claims manager, usually a director of the company, who is supported by a number of claims technicians and claims brokers.

The claims technicians are mainly concerned with entering claims information and settlement data onto the company's claims system, while the claims brokers are more involved in advising and negotiating claims.

A broker is usually notified of a potential claim by post but, unlike direct insurance claims, there is no standard claim form which the broker can examine and check. However, initially, the claims handler does try to validate the claim and also checks that premiums and premium adjustments due have been paid.

Each broker's operation has its own procedures for handling claims, but all keep in constant touch with the progress of the claim and provide assistance to clients when necessary. This may include advising the client on any documentation required, such as engineers' reports or potential loss estimates, liaising with loss adjusters and dealing with solicitors and surveyors or other appropriate specialists.

In the London Market, the development of electronic claims advice and settlement systems has led to a radical change in the claim brokers' daily routine of face-to-face claims broking. Now, the brokers spend much of their time entering claims for processing over the network systems, and reviewing and acting on claims examiners' subsequent replies.

Overseas reinsurers are still mainly advised of claims by post or, on major losses, by fax. The data input into a broker's computer system generates claim documentation, and usually includes a standard letter showing brief loss details, policy deductible and the claim recovery amount, and reinstatement premiums due if applicable. The computer system also generates entries to debit reinsurers and credit the cedant with the relevant claim settlement amounts which will appear in the periodical, often monthly, accounts.

The cedant is also issued with a copy of the computer generated claim documentation, which it returns to the broker, duly signed, by way of confirmation that the claim computation is correct.

The broker also performs certain tasks for the reinsurers, for example ensuring that the claim has been correctly computed, especially where several currencies are involved, and that hours clauses and all contract terms have been complied with.

The broker also arranges for collection of settlement amounts from clients, forwarding the applicable funds as efficiently as possible to the cedant or accounting bureau. The claims settlement service which a broker provides for its client can often be the deciding factor when a client is considering engaging the broker in future risk placements.

CLAIMS SETTLEMENT

When considering any claim, the basic principles of utmost good faith, indemnity and insurable interest apply equally, and it is the task of those responsible for the agreement of claims to ensure that these principles are adhered to.

Claims can be broadly considered under property and casualty classes of business, also referred to as short-tail and long-tail business.

On property claims, once it has been established that the loss was due to an insured peril, within the period of insurance, then the insured will normally be indemnified by the insurer.

However, in most casualty claims the decision to meet the claim is more involved, as legal liability of the insured to the third party must be established, sometimes through the courts.

In all cases, reinsurance claims examiners must first establish, as far as possible, that the loss peril is covered within the terms of the original policy. They must then satisfy themselves that the loss falls to the particular reinsurance contract under which the loss is being claimed. In determining that the claim does fall to a particular contract, the date of the loss must be examined in the light of the contract terms of cover granted by the reinsurance contract.

Although the date of a loss may be clear, the applicable contract, and so those reinsurers liable, depends on such variables as the basis of cover, including whether risks or losses have been portfolio'd out, or whether an hours clause applies.

We will consider these variables under the headings of The Basis of Cover and Contract Terms.

The basis of cover

Having established the correct date of loss, claims examiners must then establish under which reinsurance contract the loss falls. We will consider the different bases of cover of the two main types of treaties:

- excess of loss, and
- proportional.

Excess of loss

Property excess of loss contracts are issued on a risks attaching basis, or a losses occurring basis, and casualty contracts are now normally issued on a losses discovered, losses notified or claims made basis.

Risks attaching contracts cover losses on policies written new, or renewed, during the period of the reinsurance contract. The date of the loss must fall within the original policy period and not necessarily the 12-month period of the reinsurance contract. The period of the original policy is normally restricted to 12 months plus odd time, not to exceed 18 months in all.

Losses occurring contracts cover losses on policies where the original loss date falls within the period of the reinsurance contract, usually 12 months, regardless of when the original policy was issued.

Losses discovered, losses notified or claims made contracts cover casualty business where the determined loss date on the original policy—issued on a losses discovered, losses notified or claims made basis—falls within the period of the reinsurance contract.

Proportional

On property proportional treaties losses are covered on risks with an attachment date within the period of the treaty. However, the terms of the treaty may call for an unearned premium portfolio to be effected at a specific cut-off date. In this case, those risks which still have some months left to run after the agreed cut-off date must be transferred, with the appropriate premium, into the next "open" treaty year. Any claims with a loss date after the cut-off date will be settled by underwriters subscribing to the "open" treaty.

An "open" treaty is one where no outward portfolio of risks has yet been effected.

An unearned premium portfolio is normally effected with an outstanding loss portfolio.

A loss portfolio is the transfer out of known outstanding claims from one treaty to another treaty. Although the date of loss falls within the first treaty period, the outstanding loss is paid by reinsurers to the following "open" year treaty reinsurers, often at a discounted 90 per cent to allow for possible movement in reserves. The "open" year reinsurers then become liable to pay 100 per cent of the settled claim.

Some treaties allow for the transferred reserve to be reassessed in the event of a dramatic change in the loss settlement figures, so as to ensure equity between reinsurers on the two treaties.

Contract terms

Claims examiners must be fully conversant with the different contract terms which can apply to the various types of reinsurances and how they affect the compilation of any claim. In calculating losses on an excess of loss contract, the following clauses are of particular relevance when determining which contract pays.

The hours clause

Where the loss occurrence is due to one of the perils listed in the hours clause, the loss period is restricted to a number of consecutive hours. The claims examiner must be aware of this clause when checking the calculations on the possible amount recoverable under the contract. Losses occurring outside the hours period could form the basis of a further claim(s), either to same contract under the provisions of the reinstatement clause, or perhaps to another contract. In some cases the remaining claims, falling within the second loss period, must be retained net by the cedant if no reinsurance cover is available.

The reinstatement clause

Excess of loss contracts normally contain a limited number of reinstatements and the claims examiner must ensure that the claim does not exceed the available cover.

In some contracts, particularly risk excess of loss contracts, claim recovery is limited in respect of losses arising from the same loss event, despite the depth of cover otherwise available through the reinstatement clause.

LOSS RESERVING

The importance of establishing accurate reserves cannot be overstressed. However, the diverse nature of reinsurance portfolios and differences in management philosophy between any two reinsurers mean that no two companies undertake the difficult task of loss reserving in the same way.

The main participants involved in a company's loss reserving process are the claims examiners, various company managers and an actuary. The various managers involved include the claims manager, underwriting manager, underwriters, the accountant and the Chief Executive. Each person provides important input at the various stages in the reserving process.

The objective of the reserving exercise is to ensure that an adequate fund is established to cover all future liabilities of the company.

The process of reserving a company's outstanding losses may be split into three main stages. The first stage involves collecting premium and loss data and making a decision on how the risks are to be grouped and the data presented for analysis.

The second stage is to analyse the figures and identify and explain relationships and patterns which emerge and the third stage is to use the data, with the aid of subjective judgements, to make projections about ultimate settlements costs.

The need for a good computer software system or package which is flexible enough to generate meaningful statistical loss information from the data entered is of major importance if the reserving process is to be carried out effectively.

The delay factor

There are many considerations which influence the reserving of future losses and probably one of the most important is the "delay" factor.

There are two main types of delay which effect loss reserving; the delay between:

— incident and reporting, and
— reporting and settlement.

Property classes of business have relatively short periods of delay, as incidents are usually reported quite quickly and, unless the claim is disputed, settlement usually follows within a reasonable time. On property catastrophe excess of loss business most delays are due to the amount of time it takes the reinsured to group together its many small losses. A delay will inevitably occur between an initial "possible loss" advice and the actual accumulated losses reaching the excess point of the contract. Settlement of the claim is normally made promptly after the loss has breached the excess point.

Casualty claim delays can be up to 20 years or more, and it is for this reason that casualty policies are referred to as long-tail business. Casualty claims involve not only the insured and insurer, but also a "third party" to which the insured owes a duty of care. Except for the "no-fault" schemes, the insured must be legally liable for the damage caused if insurers are liable to pay any damages.

The delays between incident and reporting and then settlement of bodily injury and occupational disease claims have been the cause of much concern to reinsurers. An incident, such as exposure to asbestos, may occur many years before the disease of asbestosis manifests itself and results in a claim. Possible environmental impairment losses from pollution (EIL) are still unquantifiable by most reinsurers.

Casualty reinsurance contracts, particularly those including USA business, have moved away from a losses occurring basis to a "claims made or losses reported" basis. This helps to minimise the incident/reporting delays but can still leave long delays between reporting and final settlement.

Unfortunately, the growth in the numbers of litigation cases has resulted in backlogs for some courts, further increasing the delay period between reporting and settlement.

Litigation

The public's feeling of a right to recompense for damages suffered from someone else's action, or inaction, has led to a monumental increase in the number of tort cases. This change in social attitude to litigation has been especially noticeable in the United States of America, where awards for damages are generally higher than in any other country.

The attitudes that encourage a litigious environment influence the way insurers view a potential claim and negotiate settlement and, ultimately, reserve future losses. However, it is the unpredictability of awards that causes reinsurers the greatest concern when reserving potential third party liability claims.

Additional delay factors

On top of the initial reporting and settlement delays, reinsurers face further time delays caused by additional links in the reinsurance reporting chain.

These links could include the reinsured, the domestic reinsurance broker, the London Market broker and perhaps a retrocedant.

Additional delay factors affecting the reserving process can be found in *Financial Analysis of a Reinsurance Office* by D. Craighead.

Actuarial relief

As factors influencing the reserving process have become more complex, some reinsurers have found that they must repeatedly increase the previous amounts set aside for losses on past underwriting years. This process is often referred to as "reserve strengthening", though perhaps the term "reserve deficiency" would more accurately describe the entry.

Many claims examiners found that the accurate estimation of damages and loss adjustment expenses, on a case-by-case basis, was proving difficult, and that past experience could no longer be safely relied upon to project future loss settlement costs.

To add to the reserving problems on known losses, managements' estimates for incurred but not reported (IBNR) losses have often proved grossly inadequate, mainly due to the growth and unpredictability of third party claims. In consequence, reinsurers have looked to the actuarial profession for help in finding a more successful reserving process.

The actuary

Actuaries are skilled mathematicians with special training in probability and related techniques and they use these different techniques, based on ultimate loss settlement costs, to determine reinsurers' future losses. The appropriate method will depend on various circumstances and the mix of business in the reinsurance portfolio.

The "rule of thumb" method is still quite popular with reinsurers but other recognised techniques include the Chain Ladder method, the Bornhuetter and Ferguson method and the Craighead's modelling process method. Often, a number of alternative reserve estimates will be generated and from the various results an agreement is reached on the final reserve figure.

Each of the techniques involves an extrapolation of historical claims information and preparation of triangulations of premiums and claims, or loss ratios, by underwriting year, by development years.

Triangulations

An example of a triangulation, on a percentage loss ratio basis, is shown in Figure 26. The underwriting year, that is, the year to which the reinsurance contract is allocated, is shown on the left. The development years of each underwriting year are shown along the top, running from left to right.

The loss ratio is usually calculated by using the gross net premiums to gross paid claims, that is, the premiums and claims before reinsurance protections, e.g. proportional treaties and catastrophe excess of loss, but after acquisitions costs, e.g. commissions and brokerage.

Outward reinsurances at this initial stage are rarely included as it is the true loss patterns which the actuary is trying to identify. Also, as reinsurance protections vary from year to year, and security goes into run-off or liquidation, the loss patterns become distorted.

From the triangulation certain patterns should emerge as regards the development of losses.

In the Figure, the loss ratio after development year 4 appears to be a fair indicator of the expected ultimate loss ratio.

However, there are a number of factors which can distort these patterns for future underwriting years. A change in underwriting philosophy, a rapid increase or decrease in premium income, or inclusion of a new class of business could well upset an otherwise stable pattern.

PROJECTED LOSSES

When estimating future claims in line with recognised loss patterns, reserves for outstanding losses may be split into three types:

- Known outstanding losses,
- IBNR (Incurred but not reported) losses
- IBNER (Incurred but not enough reserved) losses.

Known outstanding losses

When a reinsurer becomes aware of a claim, or potential claim, the claims examiner enters an outstanding loss reserve figure onto the company's claim system.

The figure entered may be as per the broker's or reinsured's advice, or alternatively it may be a purely subjective figure decided upon by the claims examiner at that time.

The degree of autonomy which a claims examiner has in setting case reserves varies between companies. The amount of guidance received also varies widely, depending on the company's philosophy and its claims reserving policy.

The experience and competence of claims examiners greatly affects the claims patterns shown in any statistics gathered and the importance of consistency in loss reserving can be easily appreciated.

In establishing estimated future claim patterns, any changes in practices within the claims department should be advised to the actuary. For example, moving to an electronic network system for claims settlement and advice could dramatically speed up the recording and settlement of claims.

Underwriting Year ▼	Development Years 1	2	3	4	5	6	7	8	9	10
82	72	130	130	131	137	138	137	138	138	137
83	66	141	132	137	138	137	137	137	137	
84	75	120	119	126	122	123	122	122		
85	66	95	101	103	106	103	103			
86	67	90	99	99	99	100				
87	66	102	108	106	104					
88	77	100	101	100						
89	96	135	147							
90	94	124								
91	97									

This example shows the results of a fictitious London reinsurer's Property Proportional Treaty account. The loss ratios are calculated using paid and known outstanding losses over gross net premium income accounted on an accumulative basis each underwriting year.

Figure 26: Triangulation—Property Proportional Treaty Account (incurred % loss ratio)

IBNR losses

IBNR stands for Incurred But Not Reported and relates to losses which have been incurred by a company but which have yet to be recorded in the company's books. The provision is necessary to cover such claims as those arising from unforeseen causes, e.g. asbestos dust, and those claims under casualty policies issued on an occurrence basis, e.g. medical malpractice claims.

The IBNR reserve is not allocated to a particular policy but is a total figure applied by class, by underwriting year. The reserve is calculated by using certain actuarial techniques to project future loss trends, and once the trend has been established a provision for unforeseen disasters is added.

Crystal balls and actuarial principles work hand in hand in IBNR estimations. All actuarial techniques have their limitations, particularly when dealing with changing forces, and need a certain amount of input from the reinsurance professionals "on the ground".

However, it is perhaps more common for underwriters to take an over-optimistic view of their ultimate loss ratios—optimism being an essential characteristic of any underwriter.

Too large an IBNR provision will, of course, attract attention from the tax man.

IBNER losses

An "Incurred But Not Enough Reserved" provision is a further loss reserve on top of existing case reserves. The need for this extra reserve came about because of the deficiencies in the system of claims reporting. David Craighead, in *Financial Analysis of a Reinsurance Office*, defines IBNER as covering (in addition to normal IBNR factors):

- Claims advised to the original insurer but with insufficient information to enable the insurer to form a true picture of the severity of the loss.
- Claim outstanding advices not passed on to the reinsurer.
- Claim outstanding advices passed on to the reinsurer but so late that they cannot be included in reserve estimating.
- Claim outstanding amounts underestimated.
- Expected deterioration owing to future actual and social inflation.

By using IBNR and IBNER projections an agreement is reached on future loss figures and the insurance fund is finally established. The company's accounts can then be submitted to the appropriate insurance supervisory body for approval.

FUNDING

The collapse of a number of companies in the UK in the late 1960s alerted the state insurance regulators to the inadequate provisions made by many companies for payment of future losses, and in particular those which have not yet been reported.

The Department of Trade and Industry in the UK now takes a keen interest in how insurance and reinsurance companies calculate their provision for future losses, and schedule 4 of the company's annual DTI returns contains a valuation report to be made and signed by an appointed actuary.

Although some UK reinsurers operate a one-year basis of account, the DTI does permit them to operate a funded or three-year basis of accounting, to help alleviate somewhat the problems caused by delays in accounting of premiums and losses.

In the latter case each underwriting year is held open until the end of the third year with premiums, claims and commissions allocated to each underwriting year by reference to the date of attachment of the risks.

By the end of the third year reinsurers can calculate future losses with a far greater certainty, and hopefully the correct profit or loss can confidently be shown.

	£m	£m
FUND brought forward		10
Exchange adjustments		1
		11
Premium Income		15
		26
Less:		
Claims paid	5	
Commissions	4	
Expenses of Management	2	
		11
		15
Transfer to Profit + Loss A/c		1
FUND carried forward		14

Figure 27: Revenue Account

The insurance fund

The insurance fund relates to the liabilities for each underwriting year. In a UK reinsurance company's published set of accounts, the insurance fund appears in the revenue account. An example of a revenue account, as it may appear in a reinsurer's set of accounts, is shown in Figure 27.

Each year the fund, that is, the known outstanding losses plus IBNER and IBNR losses, is calculated on all underwriting years; call it Result A. This result is then compared to the compilation of the previous year's loss fund brought forward, plus exchange adjustments, net premium income received, claims paid and management expenses; call this Result B.

Where Result A is less than Result B, then the difference may be transferred to the company's profit and loss account.

If, however, Result B is less than Result A, then there is a shortfall in the amount needed to meet future liabilities. In this case the balance required is usually shown as a transfer from the profit and loss account.

On a three-year basis of accounting, profits from any underwriting year are only taken at the end of a period of three years from the commencement of the underwriting year. At this stage the year is referred to as "closed".

Problems may arise when the reassessment of losses on "closed" underwriting years shows that reserves have been grossly inadequate. Dividends may have been distributed to shareholders from the profits declared or additional expenses incurred on the assumption of a certain level of free reserves.

The "strengthening" of reserves usually involves a transfer of the required deficit out of the profit and loss account into the revenue account, and an injection of capital by the company's shareholders may also be required if the company's solvency margin is to remain acceptable to the authorities, and active trading is to continue.

CHAPTER 7

LONDON CLAIMS SYSTEMS

"When you start unravelling traditional taboos it's like unravelling knitting. It's hard to stop." (DUKE OF EDINBURGH, 31.5.81)

Throughout the early 1980s the need for new systems for the agreement of claims was a major source of debate in the London reinsurance market. Unfortunately, at that time, the London Market was not giving the level of claims service expected and demanded by cedants, and many began to voice their dissatisfaction.

It was time for brokers and underwriters to seriously consider a change in the traditional claims procedures.

THE PROBLEM

The main criticism of the London Market claims service was the length of time it took between making a claim and receiving a claim settlement. The reasons put forward for this delay in settling varied, but basically it was accepted that the delay was caused by the traditional procedures which existed for obtaining underwriters' agreements to settle.

The procedures involved the broker visiting the leading underwriter on the slip, with the claims file, to discuss the claim and obtain agreement to settle. The broker then visited those following reinsurers whose claims offices were situated in London, where the claim file would be examined by each reinsurer, and agreement recorded on the London Claims Collection Form (LCCF).

Those reinsurers with claims offices outside London were sent copy documentation and a form on which to notify their agreement to settle. The form, duly signed, was then returned to the broker for processing together with the LCCFs signed by London reinsurers.

The traditional face-to-face claims broking procedure in London often involved claims brokers waiting in long queues at each office to discuss the claim with an examiner. This queuing wasted time and was a very inefficient way to transact business.

The amount of time taken for claims brokers to obtain each claims examiner's agreement to settle a claim, especially where reinsurers' shares on risks were small, and their numbers large, meant it was often a physical impossibility for a broking house to obtain a speedy settlement for their client.

Once the claim had been agreed, the broker's own claims systems, and those of the processing bureaux, had to be satisfied before actual settlement could take place.

London reinsurers had developed such a bad name for claim settlements that brokers felt business was being lost, purely as a result of London's deficiencies in the claims system area.

However, reinsurers at that time saw certain advantages in retaining the face-to-face broking system, as it gave their claims examiners an opportunity to read each claims file and build up their loss negotiating experience. Indeed, the very inadequacies of the system resulted in the advantage of slowing down reinsurers' own outward cash flow.

Reinsurers were also well aware of the disadvantages of the traditional method. It generated much paperwork, was time consuming, and slowed down reinsurers' own recovery of losses.

THE SOLUTION

The disadvantages of the existing system were outweighing the advantages and brokers felt something had to be done, and quickly, if they were to retain their existing client base.

In 1986 various discussions led to a general market meeting being called to consider ways in which the London claims collection process could be substantially improved.

The result of the meeting was that LIRMA, then PSAC, agreed to consider the creation of an efficient claims handling system.

The LIRMA claims scheme which was subsequently developed is known as ELASS, the Electronic Loss Advice and Settlement System, and it operates over the electronic network of LIMNET.

ELASS included the wider concept of an electronic network system, over which brokers and reinsurers could directly communicate.

Unfortunately, the early days of ELASS were somewhat of an anti-climax, as London brokers were not fully equipped to operate the electronic claims scheme.

However, once the scheme was off the ground the enthusiasm with which companies and brokers then took it on board showed a firm commitment to advising and agreeing claims electronically, and also to the concept of electronic networking. Although over 90 per cent of LIRMA claims are now agreed over the network, the traditional system of face-to-face claims broking has not disappeared completely.

As far as the LIRMA leaders in London are concerned, they still require an initial visit from the broker and sight of the broker's claim file. Discussions and meetings with the broker also normally take place at each stage of advice and settlement.

ELASS has probably changed LIRMA claims examiners' daily routine more for following reinsurers than for the market leaders. As the assessment and agreement of a claim is normally made by the following market via the screen, a broker only visits when specifically requested to do so.

The advantages of ELASS for reinsureds, reinsurers and brokers are many, however, the greatest benefit for all must be the increase in efficiency of the London Market's claims service. The immediate and simultaneous advice of losses to reinsurers and the rapid agreement, and consequently settlement of losses, have resulted in London reinsurers regaining their competitive edge in the claims area.

Other London Market electronic claims schemes include CLAMS, the Claims Loss Advice Management System for ILU members, and CASS, the Claims Agreement and Support System for Lloyd's underwriters.

CLAIMS SYSTEMS

Claims are advised to reinsurers in a number of ways. They may be advised by a broker or, if dealing direct, by the cedant, and the advices may be sent by post, electronic mail, over the network systems of RINET or LIMNET, or advised in person by a broker at the reinsurers' claims offices.

Each reinsurance company has its own procedures and systems for entering and storing data relating to claims advices and settlements. The company may be wholly computer based, or run a combination of manual and computer based systems. The practice of maintaining a paper claims file containing copies of various reports and letters, and a computer file, is still adhered to by many reinsurers.

A large number of bespoke computerised claims systems exist within the reinsurance market and the information reinsurers receive via electronic claims systems, such as ELASS and CLAMS, may be transferred by way of standard electronic messages into these claims systems. The company's own computer database may then be interrogated for analysis of technical and financial data.

Following the LIRMA/ILU bureau merger, LPC currently operates both ELASS and CLAMS systems but plans to merge the systems, by mid-1997, into one system known as CLASS. Initially there will be no change for brokers or companies working with the systems, although the intention is to have a single set of screens within the new system. Based on this single system, LPC will then be in a position to incorporate the claims JMI agreed requirements.

The claims JMI envisages the creation of one single central electronic claim file which will contain all supporting information relating to the claim, and will be accessible electronically by all parties who have a right to see the file. All parties, including loss adjusters and attorneys, will be able to introduce any document electronically into the file. The new system will include the use of imaging, i.e. scanning of documents, and the ability to integrate the claims system with the EPS and ECA systems.

LIRMA claims

As previously mentioned, LPC currently operates two claims processing schemes for its LIRMA members; the electronic system of ELASS and the "paper driven" treaty statement scheme, which is in the process of being replaced by the electronic closing and accounting (ECA) system. The treaty statement scheme relates to the accounting aspects only of claims, whereas ELASS deals with all claims transactions, including initial loss advices.

The appropriate procedure for a claim depends on the type of risk to which the claim relates. In this regard, risks are split into two broad groups:

- — direct/facultative risks and excess of loss treaties, and
- — proportional treaties.

Claims on all classes and types of direct and facultative risks and treaty excess of loss business, including catastrophe, risk excess and stop losses, can be advised and agreed under the ELASS scheme and the remaining classes of proportional treaty claims, and claims on other "balance account" business such as lineslips are processed under the treaty statement scheme.

Once a claim settlement advice has been processed, the procedure for the payment of claims is the same for both groups of risks. All balances due are settled through LIRMA's central settlement scheme, which involves the direct debiting and crediting of members' bank accounts with the appropriate balances or refunds.

Details of the ELASS system of claims handling now follows, and the treaty statement scheme will be dealt with in the following chapter.

ELASS CLAIMS

Claims processing for LIRMA members and London brokers has changed dramatically with the introduction of the electronic agreement of claims, and for LIRMA members ELASS provides a common basic electronic processing framework which ensures the speedy and simultaneous despatch of advices and settlement requests.

Each underwriter is required to operate the system with an entirely electronic interface and all brokers must be connected to LPC, via LIMNET, in order to operate the claims system.

Whereas the former claims system dealt only with claims settlements, ELASS addresses all claims transactions from initial advice and updating reserves through to final collection. The system also permits underwriters and brokers to make on-line enquiries to the LPC computer to determine the current status of any claim transaction or sequence.

It is the brokers who are the initiators of claims onto the ELASS system and they do this either by entering the data on line into the ELASS system, or by entering it onto their own computer claims system, which by EDI is then transferred onto the ELASS system.

An outline of the ELASS on-line claims procedure is set out below, and is summarised in Figure 28.

— The broker receives a loss advice from the cedant and the broker's claims department initially checks the claim details and validity of the claim and makes up a "paper" claims file.
— When the claim details have been checked, the broker enters the claim onto the ELASS system, by various screens, and then releases the claim to the LIRMA leader.
— The broker then visits the leader with the claims file, or submits the necessary information by post.
— The leader views the claim on the screen and checks the details and, if satisfied with the broker's input, circulates the claim to following reinsurers to view and make a response.
— The leader then makes his/her own response to the claim, via the electronic screen.
— Back at the broker's office the broker then reviews all the following members' responses and satisfies any requests, until all reinsurers have accepted the claim advice or settlement.
— On a settlement request, the claim is electronically passed into LPC's central settlement scheme for payment.
— The broker receives the claim payment into its bank account and forwards it to the cedant.

System security

All subscribers to LIMNET are issued with an individual network user-id (user identification) in respect of each individual staff member authorised to use the service. Each member company and broking company must notify LPC of the user-ids allowed access to their company records, as users are only permitted to view their own company's records.

Users also have an individual password, which must be changed by them at least once a month.

Within the system many types of input and enquiry screen exist. The system details which follow are intended to provide the reader with an overall view of

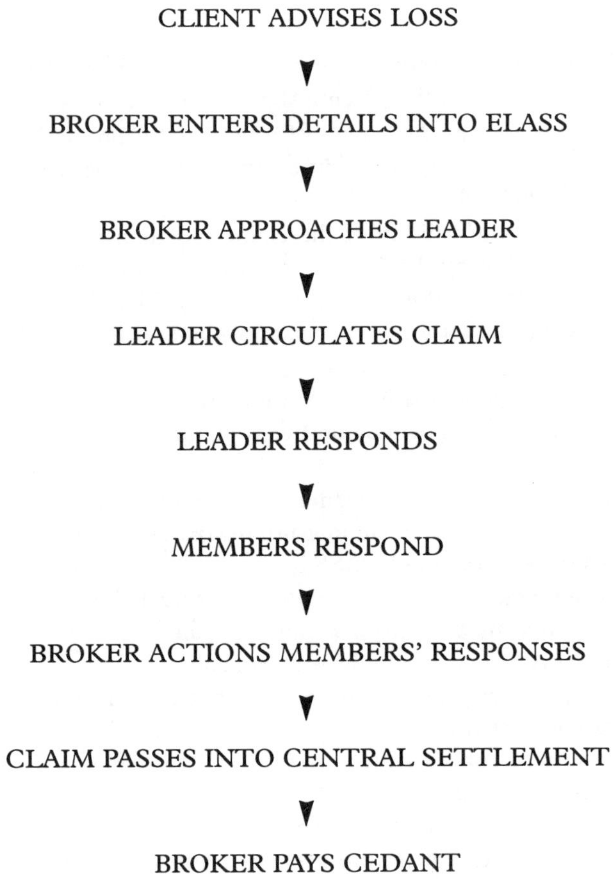

CLIENT ADVISES LOSS

▼

BROKER ENTERS DETAILS INTO ELASS

▼

BROKER APPROACHES LEADER

▼

LEADER CIRCULATES CLAIM

▼

LEADER RESPONDS

▼

MEMBERS RESPOND

▼

BROKER ACTIONS MEMBERS' RESPONSES

▼

CLAIM PASSES INTO CENTRAL SETTLEMENT

▼

BROKER PAYS CEDANT

Figure 28: ELASS procedure

how the system operates and is not intended to be fully comprehensive for input or enquiry purposes in a "live" situation.

The functions

Participants of ELASS must perform certain functions and duties if the system is to operate effectively. The functions required of broker, leader and following members are now described under:

- The broker's function
- The leader's function
- Following members' function.

The broker's function

Advising a loss

All claims advices and settlement requests on the ELASS system are initiated by the broker, as named on the placing slip or in the wording.

When the cedant advises the broker of a potential claim, either by phone, electronic mail or post, the broker first ensures that all the necessary claims details have been supplied.

The broker checks the validity of the claim and then prepares a "paper" claims file for inspection by the leader and any following reinsurer who may request sight of the claims information. The file may include such documents as original notification, adjusters' reports, and whatever information has been supplied by the cedant.

When the file is ready for the leader to inspect, the claims details may then be entered onto the broker's own computer system, or direct onto the ELASS system.

The advantage of entering the information onto the broker's own computer system is that through the use of standard messages the computer itself enters into an automatic dialogue with ELASS on the LPC computer. For the broker this has the advantage of not having to enter the same information twice, once onto ELASS and then again onto their own system.

To enter the ELASS system the broker must first be linked up, through a computer terminal, to the electronic network system of LIMNET. By using certain unique codes and passwords the broker is permitted entry to LIMNET, and a menu is subsequently displayed listing the various LIMNET facilities available.

From the LIMNET menu the broker selects LIRMA Services and the LIRMA menu is displayed. From this menu the user selects the option which gives access to the ELASS system.

On entering ELASS a further menu of options is displayed, see Figure 29, with certain of the options displayed having restricted access to brokers only.

The broker enters the code as indicated for a claims advice or settlement request and another screen is then displayed onto which the broker enters the unique market reference for the particular loss in question. The broker allocates each transaction with its own sequence number, and this number must also be input on the screen.

A series of loss information screens is then displayed for completion by the broker. Each screen may be called up by the use of different function keys as indicated at the bottom of the individual screens and, as each screen is completed, an initial validation is carried out by the system, with a final validation being carried out on completion of the final screen in the transaction sequence.

	LIRMA ELASS
	MENU SELECTION
A	ADVICE/SETTLEMENT BROKER DIRECT INPUT
B	LIRMA LEAD CIRCULATE FUNCTION
C	MEMBER MANUAL RESPONSE FUNCTION
D	CLAIM ENQUIRY (BROKER AND MEMBER)
E	MEMBER PROFILE (UPDATE AND ENQUIRY)
F	MEMBER CLAIM REFERENCE (AMENDMENT)
G	LIRMA LEAD SUMMARY
H	MEMBER RESPONSE SUMMARY
K	BROKER SUMMARY
L	U.M.R. SUMMARY
M	BROKER CHASE-UP SUMMARY
N	MEMBER CHASE-UP SUMMARY
Z	EXIT

ENTER OPTION:

Options A, K and M are for brokers only, other options are for Members.
Option L: U.M.R. stands for Unique Market Reference.

Figure 29: ELASS menu selection

The loss information screens for completion by the broker are displayed in the following order:

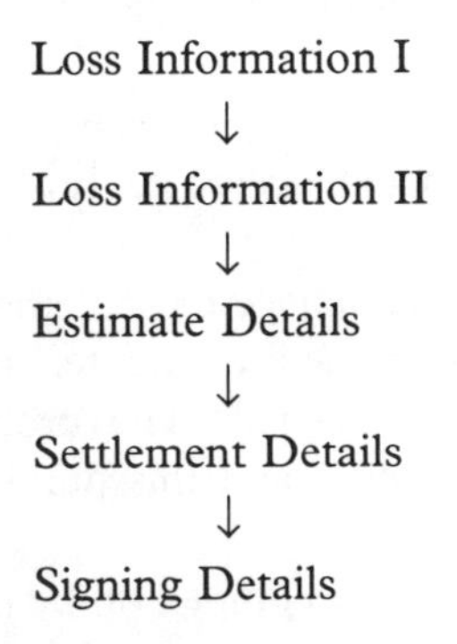

Loss Information I screen

The first loss information screen to be completed is the "Loss Information I" screen and a mock-up of the screen is shown is Figure 30. Once the details

```
COPY UCR:          — LOSS INFORMATION (1) —          COPY SEQUENCE:

BROKER CODE     :          UNQ. CLAIM REF       :
      CONTACT   :          UNQ. MARKET REF      :
       PHONE    :          SEQUENCE NO.         :
BKR CLAIM REF 1 :          BKR CLAIM REF 2      :
CLAIM TYPE      :          TRANSACTION REF      :

BKR ADVISED     :   LEAD ADV:      CAT NO:    LUNCO:       PCS:
LOSS NAME       :                               LOCATION CODE:
LOSS LOCATION:
LOSS DATE       :   TO        Q:   NARR:

DETAILS         :
OF              :
LOSS            :
                :
                :

SLIP LEAD       :                      LIRMA LEAD:
S.L. COMMENTS   :
```

Figure 30: ELASS loss information I screen

have been entered and the input is initially validated, the broker then calls up the "Loss Information II" screen, Figure 31, by use of a listed function key.

Loss Information II screen

This second screen is optional and covers details of the original policy on which the claim is made, together with the name of the lawyer and adjuster and their references, if appropriate.

```
               — LOSS INFORMATION II —
UNIQUE CLAIM REF   :            SEQ NO:          TRANS REF:

CLAIMANT           :
ORIG INSURED       :
ORIG POLICY PERIOD :       TO      NARR:
ORIG SUM INSURED   :               CCY:
ORIG DEDUCTIBLE    :               CCY:

                       CCY      AMOUNT
LOC BALANCE        :

REASSURED CLAIM REF:

LAWYER             :               REF:
ADJUSTER           :               REF:
```

Figure 31: ELASS loss information II screen

In an effort to reduce the amount of paper being circulated, facilities have been provided for brokers to supply, in free format, up to 60 lines of information.

Estimate Details screen

The next screen for completion is the "Estimate Details" screen, Figure 32, which, *inter alia*, records whether an advice or settlement transaction is being processed.

The broker can indicate this at the "TYPE" prompt, stating whether reinsurers will be receiving supporting documents in due course.

The FGU Estimate field relates to the "From the Ground Up" loss estimate, which is the 100 per cent loss regardless of slip order or deductible. If the figure is unknown, a description may be entered in the FGU Narrative field that follows it.

Settlement Details screen

If settlement is being sought, a "Settlement Details" screen, Figure 33, is displayed. On this screen, amounts relating to the paid claim, reserves retained and released, and interest, are entered. Original and settlement currencies and exchange rates must also be shown and brokers can supply settlement details in up to three currencies.

The currency must be expressed in the ISO currency code and the settlement currency must be one of the nine central settlement currencies expressed as an ISO code. Any settlement not in original currency must be settled in Sterling, US Dollars or Canadian Dollars.

```
                    — ESTIMATE DETAILS —

UNQ. CLAIM REF     :            ADV/SETT SEQ NO  :            TYPE:
AMEND DETAILS      :
ATTACHMENTS        :            CONTRACTUAL AGRMT:
LOSS PREV ADVISED NON-NETWORK:


                CCY  AMOUNT     CCY  AMOUNT     CCY   AMOUNT

FGU ESTIMATE       :
FGU NARRATIVE      :


CCY 100%  CURR EST Q 100%  PREV SET 100% O/S AMTS  Q FEES IN O/S AMT


NO. OF SIGNING DETAILS:  NO. OF LIRMA MEMBERS:  (UNCLOSED RISKS ONLY)
```

Figure 32: ELASS estimate details screen

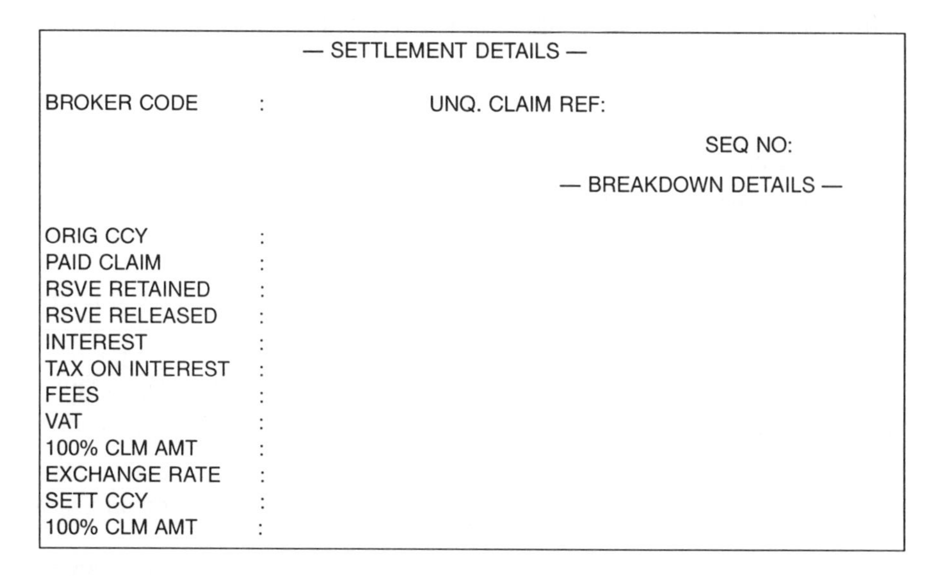

— SETTLEMENT DETAILS —

BROKER CODE : UNQ. CLAIM REF:

SEQ NO:

— BREAKDOWN DETAILS —

ORIG CCY :
PAID CLAIM :
RSVE RETAINED :
RSVE RELEASED :
INTEREST :
TAX ON INTEREST :
FEES :
VAT :
100% CLM AMT :
EXCHANGE RATE :
SETT CCY :
100% CLM AMT :

Figure 33: ELASS settlement details screen

Signing Details screen

If a settlement is being processed, the "Signing Details" screen, Figure 34, will be displayed for completion of the signing details of the contract.

On the screen a partial indicator signals that, on this sequence, the amount will only be collected from some of the LIRMA members on the contract. Payment may be in "cash" or by letter of credit as indicated by the letters C or L respectively. LOC drawings are within the ELASS scheme, however they are not settled through Central Settlement.

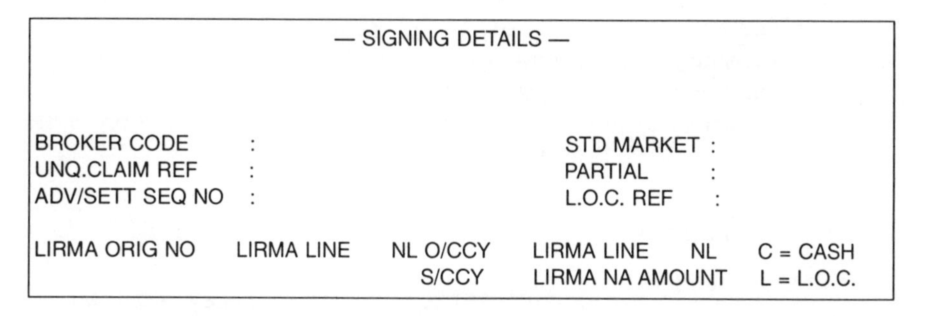

— SIGNING DETAILS —

BROKER CODE : STD MARKET :
UNQ.CLAIM REF : PARTIAL :
ADV/SETT SEQ NO : L.O.C. REF :

LIRMA ORIG NO	LIRMA LINE	NL O/CCY	LIRMA LINE	NL	C = CASH
		S/CCY	LIRMA NA AMOUNT		L = L.O.C.

Figure 34: ELASS signing details screen

If the risk has not been signed, and so no LIRMA signing number is available, the broker can only advise reinsurers of the claim and cannot request settlement. The "Signing Details" screen displayed on an advice shows only the following fields:

- — Broker Code
- — STD Market
- — UNQ. Claim Ref
- — Partial
- — ADV/SETT Seq No
- — LIRMA ORIG No
- — LIRMA Line
- — NL (number of LIRMA members involved).

The final validation across all previously completed screens is then carried out after the Signing Details screen is completed. Warnings or errors on any of the previously completed screens are highlighted for correction.

On pressing the required function key the broker releases the advice/settlement for immediate viewing by brokers within the same company, and the LIRMA leader.

The broker then approaches the leader to confirm that the loss advice details are correct. For out of town lead offices, copy documentation is posted with the appropriate form for completion.

The broker's duties

The duties of a broker operating the ELASS scheme may be summarised as follows:

- — To submit an electronic advice/settlement request to the LIRMA leader.
- — To ensure that the overall slip leader's response, if any, is made known to the LIRMA leader.
- — To ensure that all details of the LIRMA electronic advice/settlement request are agreed with the LIRMA leader.
- — To ensure prompt attention to member's requests for file or correspondence.
- — To ensure that funds received from LIRMA members are promptly passed on to the broker's client.

The leader's function

Circulating the claim

The amount of information which a leader requires to settle a claim is no less under ELASS than under the traditional system. However, the way in which the loss information is presented and captured is very different.

Immediately the broker releases the electronic loss information the file can be accessed by the leader. The leader enters the network system and the

ELASS system in the same way as outlined for a broker, using a unique set of codes and passwords.

At the ELASS menu selection, the "LIRMA Lead Summary" option permits the leader to view all the claims awaiting action. The summary display can be restricted to claims submitted by a particular broker, if required.

From the Summary screen, the selection of one of the claims listed gives the leader access to the Lead Circulate Function, as shown on the menu selection.

In practice the leader rarely selects the claim for perusal until the broker presents the claims file.

The screens may be displayed in the following sequence:

Loss Information (I) Enquiry
Lead Circulate Function
Member Response Function.

Loss Information (I) Enquiry screen

When the leader is approached by the broker, the claim in question is recalled on the screen by way of the "Loss Information (I) Enquiry" screen. This screen displays the loss information previously input by the broker in "Loss Information (I)".

First, the LIRMA company must determine that it is the correct leader on the risk for ELASS purposes. For example, if the first company on the slip indicates a conflict of interest, then the next participant on the slip, with no conflict, will then become the LIRMA leader.

The leader, in conjunction with the broker's file, then examines the data on the various screens previously completed by the broker. This ensures that all material facts relevant to the claim have been entered.

The leader cannot alter the broker's information displayed, but any comments regarding the risk or claim may be made on the Lead Circulate Function screen, which is subsequently displayed.

Lead Circulate Function screen

When the leader is satisfied with the information provided, the use of a function key calls up the Lead Circulate Function screen. It is on this screen that the claim may be rejected or circulated to the following reinsurers.

The leader completes the various fields on the screen and, if satisfied with the claim details, enters "CIRC" in the "LIRMA Lead Response" field. This indicates to LPC that the advice may be circulated to the following members for their responses.

By circulating the claim, the information on the broker's input screens, and on the lead's screen, is relayed to all members to enable them to make their individual responses.

The leader is expected to authorise LPC to circulate the advice, preferably while the broker is present, but in any event within 24 hours. To reject the claim, the leader must enter "reject" in the response field.

At this stage of the process the leader has yet to make its own response to the advice or settlement request and, therefore, immediately after the "CIRC" response which circulates the advice, a Member Response Function screen is displayed for completion. This is the same screen used by following members to indicate their individual responses to the claim sequence.

Member Response Function screen

When the leader has circulated the broker's advice or settlement request to the following members, the Member Response Function screen is displayed. This screen permits the leader to enter its own claim reference and to make its response to the claim.

The type of response depends on whether the sequence refers to a claim advice only, or a settlement request. On advices only, the response may be one of the following:

"CAA"—Claims Advice Agreed—no further action required
"INF"—Further information requested from the broker
"FIL"—Request to see the claims file or correspondence
"DIS"—The member disputes the claim.

Where the broker is requesting a settlement, the response may be INF, FIL, YES or NO. "YES" agrees to the settlement and "NO" indicates that the member is in dispute over the claim.

Once the leader has completed the screen and entered a response, the procedure for that claim sequence is completed.

The leader's duties

The duties and responsibilities of the LIRMA leader in respect of the ELASS procedure are to:

- Ensure that the company is the proper LIRMA leader as defined.
- Check that the broker advice/settlement request accurately describes the claim to following LIRMA members, adding comments as necessary.
- Validate the recommended 100 per cent reserve and to make suggested current estimates if appropriate.
- Allocate the LIRMA class of claim.
- Check that the main slip leader has agreed the advice/settlement.
- Mark the field "All U/W to See File" where appropriate.
- Indicate if the cedant is known to be in liquidation.
- Agree to the presentation of a simultaneous first advice and settlement request.

— Mark settlement requests for simultaneous reinstatement when appropriate.
— Indicate to following members that a contractual claims settlement arrangement is present on the slip.
— Indicate that the loss falls within the Small Claims Arrangement.

Following members' functions

Agreeing the claim

Once the leader has circulated the claim advice or settlement request, the following members on the risk can immediately view the particular claim sequence.

The procedure for following members entering the LIMNET and ELASS systems is the same as that described for brokers and leading companies.

When the menu selection screen is displayed, the member selects "Member Response Summary" to view and select those claims which are currently active. The summary displays the claim reference, type of advice, member's claim reference, 100 per cent amount and the response. The summary of claims can be requested by response code.

The response field on the summary indicates to the member whether a response is necessary, or whether one has already been made.

Responses may be split into two types:

- A manual case by case response
- Automatically programmed response.

Manual case by case

A manual response is one where members must, on an individual case by case basis, give their response.

In this case the response displayed on the summary is "MANUAL" and so the member must manually make a response to the sequence, via the Member Response Function screen.

Automatically programmed

A response may be made to a claim sequence automatically by the system in certain circumstances agreed by the member.

Each member supplies LPC with upper and lower automatic response levels for each claim category for each business class. The limits can apply to all brokers or be set for greater or lesser amounts for individual brokers.

The automatic responses take the following forms:

— Auto "YES" or "CAA": If the current claim estimate is below the member's automatic lower level, the claim advice or settlement is agreed.

— Auto default to manual response: If the current claim estimate is manual response between set lower and upper levels the system requires a manual response to the sequence.

— Auto "FIL": If the current claim estimate is above the upper level set, the system will automatically respond by requesting the claims file.

Automatic responses, including NFR, No Further Response, are suspended if the original current estimate increases, or if the member chooses to override the response within 24 hours, or five working days in respect of contractual claims agreements, of the original LIRMA advice/settlement request.

Automatic responses are also suspended in certain other circumstances, for example where the case is marked "All U/W to See File", or the cedant is in liquidation.

The automatic response profile of each member is interrogated by the system using the Broker code, Business Class and Claims category input by the leader. If no profile exists for a particular category, the Response field is preset to "Manual".

Following Member Response Function

By selecting individual items from the Summary screen, the Member Response Function screen is displayed. The member may also recall the specific advice, or settlement request, by the Member Manual Response Function option of the menu selection screen.

Regardless of the automatic member response allocated, members may respond manually to a claim. It may also become necessary to alter the automatic response or alter a previous response, i.e. "FIL" to "CAA".

Following reinsurers must respond within 10 working days to each loss advice received.

When the positive acceptance of all the members has been made, the settlement will be transferred into the existing LIRMA claims system. The settlement is then allocated a LIRMA signing date and number, which is displayed on all enquiry screens.

ENQUIRY FACILITIES

All brokers and members can make on-line enquiries to the computer system, via the network, to determine the current status of any claim on which they have an involvement.

Members may also view the responses made by other members on claims on which they also participate.

The enquiry option is shown on the menu selection screen under "CLAIM ENQUIRY".

CHAPTER 8

PROPORTIONAL TREATY CLAIMS

"It is to be noted when any part of this paper appears dull, there is a design in it." (SIR RICHARD STEELE, 1672–1729)

PROPORTIONAL TREATY CLAIMS

This chapter deals with the ways and means by which paid and outstanding claims on proportional treaties, including lineslips and binding authorities settled on a balance basis, are advised and processed in the London Market.

As most proportional treaty arrangements do not include the need for reinsurers' prior agreement to settle losses, except in certain circumstances, losses are automatically offset against premiums due.

This "blind" settlement of losses as part of the partnership concept associated with the successful operation of a proportional treaty means that the reinsurers must rely heavily on the competence of the cedant when it comes to settling claims.

Reinsurers must also put their trust in the cedant to allocate losses to the correct treaty year and to precisely calculate the portion of the loss applicable to the treaty. In addition, reinsurers must rely on their "partners" to promptly and accurately advise all outstanding losses and to inform them of all paid and outstanding losses attributable to any one loss occurrence.

ACCOUNTING FOR LOSSES

The accounts that a cedant prepares should include entries relating to the loss provisions as shown on the slip or in the treaty wording.

The treaty may provide for a cash loss, a preliminary loss advice, loss reserves or a loss portfolio and, before processing the account, the broker and reinsurer must check that all the relevant claims figures and details have been provided.

From time to time, further information on the paid and outstanding losses advised may be requested by reinsurers. Questions asked may include: Are any catastrophe/event losses included in the paid and outstanding loss figures supplied?, or, Has a previously advised outstanding loss been included in the total claims settlement figure?

Outstanding losses

Many cedants are aware of the importance to reinsurers of accurate and timely advice of outstanding claim advices for the estimation of reinsurers' own reserves. Others, however, are less aware and accommodating, supplying the necessary figures a year or two late, or indeed, not until they are heavily pressed for the information.

The accurate identification and recording of major losses within the total outstanding loss amounts advised under a treaty is also very important to reinsurers. The very nature of reinsurance means that an individual loss or loss event will be advised from a number of sources and, for their own recovery purposes, reinsurers need to keep track of all claims received on that one loss occurrence.

To facilitate the accumulation of the individual claims, the reinsurer must first identify all settled or reserved, individual or event claim amounts, under the treaty. Having identified the amounts applicable to the event, the reinsurer can then allocate its unique event code to each settled or reserved claims entry.

In this way, and with the aid of a suitable computer programme, the accurate and efficient accumulation of event losses within a proportional treaty is possible. This timely accumulation enables reinsurers to make an early recovery against their own risk or catastrophe excess of loss protections.

Although the terms of most treaties clearly cater for regular advices of outstanding or unsettled claims on major losses, the provision is all too often ignored.

However, reinsurers may specifically request outstanding loss information through:

- loss bordereaux, and
- preliminary loss advices.

Loss bordereaux

Under the terms of the treaty, the cedant may be required to provide a statement, or bordereau, of outstanding losses at regular intervals.

The bordereau is normally submitted with each periodic account and shows the name of the loss, date of loss, period, amount of policy and loss estimate.

Preliminary loss advices

It is common to find a preliminary loss advice provision in proportional treaties. This provision calls for the cedant to advise reinsurers immediately of any loss which exceeds or may exceed a certain predefined limit.

The delay in the reporting of outstanding losses on treaties has caused, and continues to cause, reinsurers concern. When underwriters are considering renewal terms of a treaty, outstanding losses play an important part in the decision process. In addition, inadequate recording of future liabilities due to incompetent reporting of outstanding losses can have dire consequences for reinsurers.

Although mainly resisted by reinsurers, it is sometimes only through the provision for outstanding loss reserves that reinsurers are able to keep track of their future liabilities.

REPORTING LOSSES

Paid and outstanding

There is no universally accepted proportional treaty account for reporting losses, however the Standard Reinsurance Account format is increasingly being used within the London Market.

The Standard Reinsurance Account is shown in full in Figure 23 in Chapter 5, but for ease of reference, the claims items in the various sections are repeated here in Figure 35.

The sections are headed:

(A) Cash Account
(F) Reserve Interest Breakdown
(G) Claims Breakdown
(H) Individual Loss Information
(I) Outstanding Claims Information
(L) Narrative Information.

The main claims items within each of these sections are now discussed.

(A) Cash Account

The claims items shown in the cash account represent claims to be paid or refunded in that particular periodic account. A breakdown of the items, and any additional information, is shown in Sections (G), (H), (I) and (L) of the account.

Nett claims (item 010)

The nett claims amount shown against item 010 is the result of the various entries as listed in section (G) Claims Breakdown, discussed later.

(A) CASH ACCOUNT

010 Nett Claims
011 Claim Reserve Retained
012 Claim Reserve Released
013 OCA Retained
014 OCA Released
015 Claim Portfolio Incoming
016 Claim Portfolio Outgoing
017 Reinsurance Recoveries

(F) RESERVE INTEREST BREAKDOWN

101 Claims Reserve Interest

(G) CLAIMS BREAKDOWN

110 Paid Claims
111 Paid Refunds
112 Cash Loss
113 Cash Loss Contra Entry
114 Nett Claims

(H) INDIVIDUAL LOSS INFORMATION

130 Date of Loss
132 PCS. Catastrophe Number
133 Name of Loss
134 Nature of Claim
135 Loss Details
136 Claim Reserve Retained
137 Claim Reserve Released
138 OCA Retained
139 OCA Released
140 Claim Portfolio In
141 Claim Portfolio Out
142 Reinsurance Recoveries
143 Claim Reserve/OCA Interest
144 Outstanding Losses
145 Paid Claims
146 Paid Refunds
147 Cash Losses
148 Cash Loss Contra Entry

(I) OUTSTANDING CLAIMS INFORMATION

160 Balance of Claim Reserve
161 Balance of OCA
162 Outstanding Loss Amount
163 Adjusted Outstanding Loss Amount

(L) NARRATIVE INFORMATION

500 Free Format Information

Figure 35: claims items on SRA

Claim reserves/OCAs (items 011 to 014)

A claim reserve deposit is an amount retained from reinsurers in respect of all claims notified on the treaty, but not yet paid.

The initial reason for cedants retaining loss reserves was to safeguard themselves against reinsurers not meeting their obligations under a treaty. Currently they are mainly imposed due to local conditions and legislation, more than any other reason.

There are three possible methods by which loss reserves may be retained by the cedant:

- cash in account
- outstanding claims advance—OCA
- letter of credit—LOC.

Cash in account

Some cedants retain an outstanding loss reserve on a quarterly basis, and release the reserve the following quarter when a new reserve deposit is calculated and retained in the account.

The entries applicable to the claim reserves retained are shown in the Cash Account section in Claims Reserve Retained, item 011, and the claim reserves released are shown in Claims Reserve Released, item 012.

In some cases, the appropriate reserves may be retained each quarter, but not released for a further 12-month period.

On certain treaties the wording may only call for a loss reserve to be established on termination of the treaty, or when a reinsurer declines to renew the treaty.

Reserves are usually retained at 90 per cent of the known outstanding losses to allow for a degree of saving in the final settlement figures.

It is normal for a cedant to pay a set rate of interest to reinsurers on the reserves retained, and Section (F) item 101 shows interest due when the account includes a release of reserves.

Outstanding claims advance

An outstanding claims advance is an advance of cash, made by the reinsurer, to cover known outstanding losses on a reinsurance contract. The advance may sometimes be made under a trust agreement to a third party such as a bank.

It has become common practice to deal with an OCA on a proportional treaty in the same way as a cash reserve, and account for the advance in the normal cash account. Here, the OCAs are always dealt with on a revolving basis and the OCA amount released, OCA Released, item 014, always equals the amount previously retained in OCA Retained, item 013.

In many cases losses covered under an OCA, either retained in the cash account or set up under a trust agreement, are settled in the normal cash account without regard to the established OCA. Although the OCA amount should be adjusted following a settlement it often remains intact and is only recalculated at renewal date, when it is released and the new adjusted OCA is retained in the same periodical account.

Letter of credit

A letter of credit (LOC) is a clean, irrevocable, unconditional instrument issued by a bank on behalf of a reinsurer, which can be drawn down to cover a reinsurer's liabilities under a reinsurance agreement.

Although the setting up and drawing down of LOCs is outside the standard cash accounting process, the balance of undrawn amounts should be shown in the accounts under Section (I) Outstanding Claims Information and clearly marked LOC.

As with an OCA, it is common practice on a proportional treaty to settle losses in the periodic account without drawing down on the LOC. In theory the LOC should be adjusted once the reinsurer has settled, but in practice the LOC often remains in force for the full amount and is recalculated at renewal time.

Claim portfolios (items 015/016)

A claim portfolio is the transfer of known liabilities on one underwriting year to the next "open" year. It may be effected after 12, 24 or 36 months, or even longer after the inception date of the treaty. The longer the period the greater the accuracy of the estimated outstanding liabilities will be. The portfolio is often calculated at 90 per cent of the outstanding loss amount, in line with outstanding loss reserves retained.

Item 015 shows the incoming portfolio from a previous underwriting year and normally should be identical to the outgoing claims portfolio from the previous underwriting year. Any differences which do occur should be explained, e.g. where a 90 per cent quota share treaty is renewed on a reduced quota share percentage.

As an incoming portfolio represents outstanding liability, item 161 in Section (I) Outstanding Loss Information should be completed and the 90 per cent loss portfolio figure should be grossed up to 100 per cent to reflect reinsurers' total liability.

The outgoing claims portfolio which transfers out of the treaty all known outstanding claims is shown in item 016. As the entry removes all outstanding losses from the treaty, item 162 in Section (I) Outstanding Loss Information, should show a "NIL" entry.

The outgoing claims portfolio on the closed year should be accounted at the same time as the incoming portfolio on the following open underwriting year.

Reinsurance recoveries (item 017)

It is not unusual for a cedant to effect a reinsurance for joint account protection of its reinsurers. It may purchase facultative reinsurance on a particularly hazardous risk ceded to the treaty, or a catastrophe excess of loss reinsurance to protect reinsurers and the treaty results.

Item 017 relates to any recoveries due to reinsurers as a result of a protection which has been purchased for reinsurers. The premium due for the protection is entered in Section (A) Cash Account, item 008.

(G) Claims Breakdown

The nett claims amount shown in item 010, Section (A) Cash Account, is made up of various items as set out in Section (G) Claims Breakdown.

The Claims Breakdown section includes entries for paid claims, refunds and cash losses. The Paid Claims, item 110, is self-explanatory and, the Paid Refunds, item 111, refers to salvage and recoveries due to reinsurers.

Cash loss (items 112/113)

Most proportional treaties contain the provision that, should a paid claim under the treaty exceed a defined limit, the claim will be paid by reinsurers in advance of the periodic account.

Where the cash loss(es) are paid in advance of the account, often by Special Settlement, but are also included under Paid Claims, item 110, the cash loss amount should be shown in Cash Loss Contra Entry, item 113. This entry reverses the losses previously paid and shown again in item 110.

If, however, the cash loss(es) are settled in the standard account they should be included in the entry Cash Loss, item 112.

In either case, full details of each individual cash loss must also be shown under Section (H) Individual Loss Information, either under Cash Losses, item 147, or Cash Loss Contra Entry, item 148.

(H) Individual Loss Information

The items shown in Section (H) relate to entries included in Section (A), Section (G), or Section (I), but only in respect of individual loss information.

Date of loss (item 130)

In order that reinsurers may identify correctly a particular loss, the loss date, or, on an occurrence loss, the "from" and "to" dates of the loss period should be advised.

PCS Cat. number (item 132)

Where a unique claim number has been allocated by the Property Claims Service (PCS), it should be entered in item 132.

If details of more than one individual loss are to be entered in the same account, the items in Section (H) may be repeated as required.

(I) Outstanding Claims Information

This section of the SRA relates to the total of outstanding losses and balance of reserves at the end of the periodic account.

Balance of claims reserve/OCA (items 160/161)

These items relate to the balance of reserves still retained by the cedant following the release or drawing down of current reserves.

Outstanding loss amount (item 160/161)

The importance to reinsurers of recording accurate outstanding loss information has already been mentioned, and it is in this section of the SRA that the reserve amounts should be entered.

The item can be an amount, "NIL" or "NAD" (None Advised), but when NAD frequently appears in the account it needs to be questioned by the reinsurer.

Adjusted outstanding loss amount (item 163)

This item shows an adjusted total of outstanding losses reflecting cash loss collections or additional information received subsequent to the periodic account.

(L) Narrative Information (item 500)

This section can be used to provide reinsurers with any additional information that may be helpful to them.

The way in which LPC checks and processes proportional claims is now considered.

CLAIMS ACCOUNTING AT LPC

LIRMA members

The processing of LIRMA members' proportional treaty claims will be included in the electronic closing and accounting system currently being developed for proportional treaty business. However, at this stage, proportional treaty claims continue to be processed under the paper-based treaty statement scheme, as outlined in Chapter 5.

Where claims arise as part of a periodic treaty statement, they are accepted by LPC without proof of prior agreement by company members. However, the words "Claims Authority" appear together with the signature of an authorised signatory in the top left-hand corner of the treaty statement when:

— There is a loss advice provision incorporated in the treaty.
— The treaty statement is in respect of or includes a cash loss.

The broker's signature confirms that the broker has complied with the provisions of any loss advice clause in the treaty. In this way, the bureau also puts the onus on brokers to ensure that they have complied with the particular requirements imposed by individual companies.

Any breach of these requirements is dealt with by the companies concerned, which may initially mean objecting to the treaty statement advice and having it withdrawn from central settlement. This action is then usually followed up by discussions with the broker concerned.

Technical checks

In addition to the mathematical checks which LPC carries out, LPC also compares loss amounts shown on the treaty statement with those advised by the cedant, also checking that entries are compatible with the slip conditions. In addition, technicians ensure that reserve accounts are properly processed in accordance with slip requirements.

Claim files on individual losses are not kept by the bureau, but there are a number of enquiries which LPC may make on behalf of reinsurers.

If, for example, major losses are suspected but not included within Sections (H) and (I) of the account, LPC may request the broker to supply details of catastrophe and other major losses, both settled and outstanding, under the treaty.

Where a loss figure on the treaty statement looks large enough to include a possible cash loss or preliminary loss advice, the loss figure will be queried with the broker.

Binding authorities

Accounting entries on binding authorities, lineslips and covers, settled on a balance basis, are processed under the treaty statement scheme.

Whenever claims are included in the treaty statement, they are dealt with in the same way as any proportional treaty, the claims authority on the reverse of the treaty statement being completed with the broker's stamp and authorised signature. This authorisation indicates that the broker has obtained the required companies' agreements to the claim and has complied with any loss advice conditions contained in the binding authority.

In general, a cedant's original account, preliminary loss advice documentation and loss bordereaux supplied by the cedant, is not passed on by the bureau to their members and it is the broker's responsibility to forward the documentation direct to reinsurers.

THE ELECTRONIC LETTER OF CREDIT

"ELECT"

The traditional procedure for the agreement of letters of credit, as outlined in Chapter 3, has been time consuming for brokers and reinsurers alike. So it was that the London Market and Citibank jointly developed the Electronic Letter of Credit Transactions scheme, "ELECT".

The original aim of ELECT was to improve the competitiveness of the London insurance market by automating the delivery and authorisation of LOCs between the London Market and Citibank. The scheme is available to

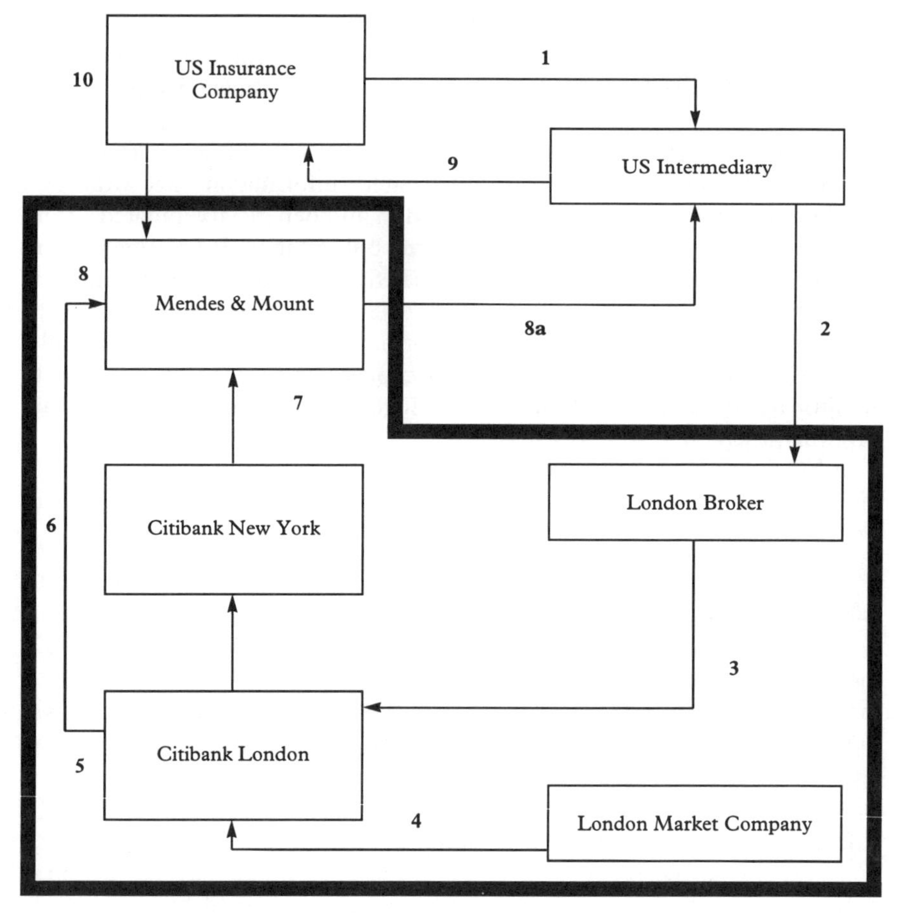

Figure 36: London Market "ELECT" LOC Scheme

network users of LIMNET, RINET and IBM MNS (Management Network Service).

In addition to outstanding losses, ELECT also handles UPRs (unearned premiums reserves) and OCAs (outstanding claims advances).

The scheme was developed in two phases. In the completed phase I, details of new LOCs, increases, reductions and amendments, are supplied to London reinsurers from London brokers to Citibank ELECT services, using standard EDI messages.

Through a series of online screen displays, reinsurers agree the LOC requests via their terminals, and may review historical LOC details and information. Figure 36 outlines phase I of the scheme shown within the bold line.

Phase II, expected to be fully operational in the near future, relates to the electronic delivery of beneficiary originated information, i.e. drawings, reinstatements, and reductions (both London and beneficiary initiated), from Mendes & Mount Electronic Claims Level Information Processing System (ECLIPS), through the Citibank ELECT System, to reinsurers and brokers.

Citibank also provides an electronic information service for all parties to the LOC. Cedants, intermediaries, London brokers and reinsurers are able to monitor the status of each LOC from a single database (source), and obtain LOC history dating back to 1981.

ELECT services are also available to cedants and reinsurers who deal direct with each other on certain business and do not use the services of a broker.

CHAPTER 9

INACTIVE REINSURERS—THE RUN-OFF

"To be, or not to be, that is the question . . ." (WILLIAM SHAKESPEARE, *Hamlet*)

INACTIVE REINSURERS

The 1990s have been a difficult time for reinsurers in the London Market, evidenced by the number of companies and syndicates which have ceased actively underwriting.

The reasons why the shareholders of a company close down their reinsurance operation are many and varied, ranging from insolvency of the company and forced closure to simply an overall change in company strategy.

One of the main reasons leading to closure must surely be poor underwriting results. When bad results are coupled with inadequate reserving, the paid-up capital of the company is eventually reduced to a level which is insufficient to enable further underwriting to continue.

Whatever the reasons for "pulling out" of the reinsurance market, the decision to do so has long-ranging effects on both cedants and brokers, at home and abroad.

As regards the brokers, they may well suffer on two accounts, often losing an existing client as well as a potential reinsurer with which to place future business.

Cedants, on the other hand, not only lose a potential reinsurer, but slow recoveries may lead to major cash flow problems for their company.

In addition, the danger of an insolvent company causing the collapse of other reinsurers in the market, in a domino-like effect, may be a real problem.

There are three possible paths a company can take when it ceases actively underwriting and they are:

- liquidation
- portfolio reinsurance
- run-off.

Liquidation

In the UK the government department responsible for regulating and supervising the business of insurance and reinsurance is the Insurance Division of the Department of Trade and Industry (DTI).

The DTI may agree to a petition to wind up a company if that company

- — is unable to pay its debts, that is, the company was insolvent at the date of its last balance sheet
- — has failed to satisfy an obligation under the Insurance Companies Act 1982
- — has failed to keep proper accounting records and the DTI is unable to ascertain its financial position.

The petitioning parties on a winding-up order may be the creditors of the company or the company itself or, although in practice rarely encountered, the DTI. In most cases the application is made on the grounds that the company is "unable to pay its debts".

Basically, under the winding-up order, the courts appoint an Official Receiver, who appoints a liquidator to manage the winding-up of the company.

The liquidator is a licensed insolvency practitioner, whose job is to realise assets, agree claims and pay dividends to creditors. The liquidator must identify the causes of the insolvency, and also has a duty to investigate the company's affairs with particular reference to the pre-liquidation activities of the company's directors.

There is an alternative to liquidation for insolvent companies and this is to propose a Scheme of Arrangement.

Scheme of Arrangement

It is common practice, as an alternative to liquidation, for the directors or the provisional liquidator of a reinsurance company to propose a Scheme of Arrangement. The number of schemes proposed for insurance companies has increased dramatically as liquidation is now often considered an inappropriate and expensive way of dealing with an insolvent insurer.

The scheme basically means a reconstruction of a reinsurance company's assets and liabilities profile. However, establishing a list of creditors and debtors is not an easy or quick task, especially where business has been written through a number of different brokers at home and abroad. This task is also made more difficult as most reinsurance companies maintain their accounts at broker level rather than at cedant level.

A proposed scheme requires the consent of the courts and 75 per cent in value, or over 50 per cent in number, of creditors, before it may proceed.

The main advantage of a scheme is that it permits greater flexibility when considering what action could be taken to protect the interests of creditors. It also gives an opportunity for the orderly realisation of assets with a view to paying an early dividend. The disadvantage of the scheme is that the powers available to a liquidator to pursue actions against directors are less.

As the dividend paid is inevitably less than 100 per cent of the amount due to cedants this can cause problems when the reinsurers make their own recoveries from their reinsurers, despite recent case law which now confirms the right to this full recovery.

Where the company has a portfolio which includes casualty business the scheme may run for a number of years. In this situation, the ultimate aim of the liquidator is to crystallise future losses by actuarial methodology so that dividends may be paid to creditors.

Under the terms of the scheme, the administrator continues to process the technical and financial information until expiry of the run-off.

Portfolio reinsurance

When a reinsurance company no longer wishes to continue underwriting it may be in a position to retrocede the entire portfolio of its business to another reinsurer.

In some cases the premium charged by the retrocessionaires may be sufficient to pay for all eventual liabilities, and leave some margin of profit for the shareholders.

As many underwriters have withdrawn from reinsuring whole account portfolios of business, mainly due to the problem of accurately estimating IBNR losses, this course of action may not be a real option for most companies.

Approval of the DTI may also be required for the transfer of liability. However, if the option to reinsure is available, the company still remains liable for its claims if its retrocessionaire fails to pay out for whatever reason.

Run-off

The DTI may withdraw a company's authorisation to transact business while still permitting the company to "run off" its liabilities under existing policies.

Withdrawal of the authorisation may be at the direction of the Secretary of State on the grounds that the company has failed to comply with an obligation under the Insurance Companies Act 1982. Alternatively, the withdrawal may be at the company's own request.

Under a run-off the company continues to meet its liabilities as and when they occur, and this option to "run off" a portfolio has been taken by many of the London reinsurance companies over the years.

A UK company can continue to manage itself in a run-off situation as long as there are sufficient net assets to match the solvency requirement. If the net assets are insufficient at any future date, then the company will be put into liquidation or managed under an agreed Scheme of Arrangement.

The length of time it takes for all liabilities to be settled by a company is dependent on the type of business previously underwritten by the company. If the portfolio includes long-term casualty business, such as medical malpractice, a run-off period of 20 years plus is possible.

Run-offs may be carried out

- in-house, or by
- run-off administrators.

In-house

When running off the portfolio, the company may decide to use its remaining accounts and claims staff to process the existing business.

However, shareholders must prove to the DTI that future liabilities and ongoing overheads, such as salaries, rent, lighting etc, can be met from its existing reserves.

Often the "ex-employees" will form a separate run-off company, which is then engaged by the run-off company's shareholders to manage the portfolio.

Apart from the moral aspect, shareholders may feel that there is a cost advantage in using staff who are "au fait" with the company's computer system and often complex reinsurance protections.

Run-off administrators/consultants

The alternative to using an in-house team to run off all liabilities is to use the services offered by a run-off administrator, or consultant.

The administrator is responsible for processing the company's existing portfolio and there is no assumption of liability from the run-off company.

As with any situation, there are advantages and disadvantages for shareholders in running off a company's liabilities.

Advantages of run-off

The main advantage of running-off is that the shareholders keep control of the company. This helps them to maintain their reputation in the insurance market, particularly important if they continue to be involved in the insurance industry.

The cost of running off a portfolio is also relatively cheap, and shareholders may benefit from the future use of any assets which remain after all liabilities have been settled.

Disadvantages of run-off

The main disadvantage of running off a portfolio is that it takes a long time, and shareholders may wish to put the past behind them and concentrate on other areas of investment.

Also, in order for the run-off to work, the shareholders must provide, and be willing to provide, financial backing for any shortfalls in the solvency margin.

Some shareholders may feel that the company could become a bottomless pit as far as future investment is concerned, and so would rather "cut their losses" sooner rather than later.

THE RUN-OFF ADMINISTRATORS

The majority of services provided by administrators in the London Market are those required by an inactive company to run off its existing portfolio.

However, most administrators are not solely involved in processing run-off portfolios, and usually provide services to on-going operations too. These services may include renewal audits, fund reviews and arbitration and underwriting services.

The main activities of an administrator, for inactive and active companies, may be divided into three distinct divisions as shown in Figure 37:

- Administration services (1)
- Special services (2)
- Information technology (IT) (3).

Administration (1)

In a run-off situation, although the shareholders may have "closed down" the operating divisions of their company and have no staff or premises to contend with, there still exist certain day-to-day duties which must be performed.

Not only must the technical and financial processing continue to be carried out, but the run-off company's affairs must also be managed. This includes preparing the statutory returns to the DTI, engaging accountants to audit the company's accounts and reporting to shareholders.

Special services (2)

Special Services, or Division 2, mainly relates to the claims function and the reduction and control of future liabilities.

The main objective of most shareholders in a run-off situation is to settle all its liabilities in the shortest time possible. Therefore, administrators tend to become heavily involved in discussions on commuting liabilities on inward business with cedants, and also on outward reinsurances with retrocessionnaires.

Litigation and arbitration services are also provided by administrators as they usually act on behalf of their client in any disputes which arise.

Information technology (3)

Maintaining an up-to-date computer system to process the volume of transactions handled is important in managing a run-off company. In some cases

1
ADMINISTRATION SERVICES

Corporate Management

Technical/Financial Services

DTI Returns

Reporting

Technical Back-Up

Underwriting

2
SPECIAL SERVICES

Claims

Audits of Accounts

Inspections

Commutations

Portfolio Analysis

Arbitration

Fund Reviews

1
INFORMATION TECHNOLOGY (IT)

In-House Computer Support

External IT Services

Figure 37: main divisions within an administrator's company

information may need to be transferred from the clients existing, and perhaps outdated, computer system onto the consultant's system.

Also, the reinsurance market worldwide is becoming increasingly reliant on the passing and receiving of information over electronic networks. It is, therefore, imperative for those shareholders wishing to minimise costs, that the processing of the premiums and claims can continue to be dealt with in the most efficient way.

THE RUN-OFF PROCESS

The main aspect of running off a reinsurance company's liabilities, whether performed in-house or by a run-off administrator, is the efficient management of the share capital and insurance fund of the company.

The first step in the run-off process is to carry out a comprehensive review of the company with a view to drawing up a business plan. This plan will include, *inter alia*, current and future underwriting results, cash flow, revenue income and expenses forecasts.

The very nature of reinsurance business means that regular reviews of the portfolio need to be carried out. New information is constantly coming to hand and, as outstanding reserves become settled claims, a revision of the IBNR figure may well be necessary.

Some of the difficulties which may be experienced in running off a portfolio of risks are now considered.

Run-off difficulties

Some of the problems which a company may encounter in a run-off are now:

- loss of goodwill and confidence
- acceleration of claims reporting
- retention of funds by brokers
- offsets
- LOC drawings.

Loss of goodwill and confidence

In order that the company can run off its business in an orderly fashion it will need to maintain goodwill with all its debtors, creditors and brokers.

Any loss of goodwill and lack of confidence in management to settle claims as quickly and efficiently as possible will invariably lead to cedants and brokers retaining funds due to the company, so causing cash flow problems.

One way in which loss of goodwill may arise is due to the company deciding to cease paying claims for a prolonged period of time, on the basis that management is reviewing the company's figures.

Ceasing to be a member of an accounting bureau, thus slowing down claim payments and resulting in higher processing costs for the broker, may also lead to loss of goodwill and lack of confidence in prompt settlement of future claims payments.

Acceleration of claims reporting

The natural reaction of a cedant on hearing that one of its reinsurers has ceased underwriting is to look closely at its potential claims recovery position. Bearing in mind that at any future stage the "run-off" may turn into a "liquidation", cedants' claim settlement requests and updated and new outstanding claims advices tend to accelerate following this review.

This increase in advices may also be used to justify the non-payment of balances due to the reinsurer, say in cases where premiums are due or, indeed, where the "cedant" is also a reinsurer of the run-off company, as is frequently the case in the reinsurance market.

The acceleration of claims reporting leads to further inroads being made into the company's reserves and capital, pushing it that bit sooner into possible insolvency.

Retention of funds by brokers

Brokers often feel that initially, to protect their clients' interest, they should stop paying balances due to a company in run-off.

However, brokers are only creditors of the reinsurer as regards monies owed to them, i.e. brokerage, and any funds should, in theory, be passed on or back to the appropriate company.

To make things more complicated, the broker may have funded monies on behalf of its client, now in run-off. Funding is where a broker pays one party monies which are due from another (client), but which the broker has not yet collected.

The broker will, therefore, be trying hard to rectify this situation, knowing that if the run-off company subsequently goes into liquidation, its position as regards the recovery of the funded amounts may be in some doubt.

Offsets

If a cedant has lost confidence in a run-off company's ability to meet its liabilities in the usual timespan, it will be keen to offset any amounts due between itself and the company in run-off.

In the offset calculation, the cedant may not only include the current debit and credit situation, but may also take into account any payments which it believes will become due from the reinsurer. This could include known outstanding losses which may not become payable, and so recoverable from the reinsurer, for some years.

Where the cedant is also one of the run-off company's reinsurers, who is also including outstanding liabilities in its calculations, it is easy to understand how confrontation between parties can arise, and how the agreement of balances could take some time.

As offset balances can take time to compute, offsetting can drastically reduce, and in some cases stop, a run-off company's cash flow, especially in the early stages of run-off.

LOC drawings

If the run-off company has set up letters of credit to cover outstanding losses under a reinsurance treaty, it may find that the various beneficiaries will draw down the funds as soon as they are aware that the company has gone into run-off.

Although the beneficiary may not have paid the claims, the premature drawing of the LOC is legitimate if the funds are placed in an escrow account where interest can be earned for the benefit of the reinsurer.

However, even if the drawing was possibly improper, it is unlikely that the company would have the resources or inclination to litigate against the beneficiary.

Where drawings have taken place, the periodical accounts must be closely checked by the accounting technicians to ensure that, as the outstanding claims become paid, these paid claims are not shown as due for payment in the treaty statement.

Concluding the run-off

One day, the run-off process of a reinsurance company must come to an end. This may either be through:

— natural expiry
— transfer of liabilities, or
— liquidation.

Under natural expiry and transfer of liabilities the remaining assets, if any, will then be free from the company to be fully utilised by shareholders for other activities.

Under a liquidation all assets of the company will be distributed, and any uncollected balances will appear as a bad debt provision in its creditors' accounts.

APPENDIX 1

FACULTATIVE SLIP DETAILS

TYPE:	Facultative Excess—All Risks
FORM:	Slip Policy
INSURED:	The Steel Band Company of Trinidad and Tobago Limited
REINSURED:	Class A Reinsurance Co Limited
PERIOD:	12 months at 1 January 1996
INTEREST:	All Real and Personal Property on the Insured
SUM INSURED:	Limit: TT$ 90,000,000 each and every loss Excess of: TT$ 10,000,000 each and every loss
SITUATION:	Trinidad and Tobago, as original
CONDITIONS:	Full Reinsurance Clause Terms and Conditions as original
PREMIUM:	45% of Original Net Premium
BROKERAGE:	10%
INFORMATION:	Survey Report dated November '95 seen by Underwriters. Total values TT$ 100 million. Clean 5 years.

APPENDIX 2

SURPLUS SLIP DETAILS

(Courtesy of Insurance Institute of London)

C.A.B. INSURANCE BROKERS LIMITED in conjunction with B.C.D. Insurance Brokers Limited.

REFERENCE NO:	U017084065230
REASSURED:	A.B.C. INSURANCE COMPANY LIMITED, VIENNA, AUSTRIA
PERIOD:	Continuous contract, shares hereon from 1 January 1985 subject to three months notice of cancellation at 31 December in any year.
CLASS:	In respect of Direct, Commercial and Industrial Fire and Extended Perils business written or renewed by the Reassured, excluding Earthquake shock and Fire following.
TERRITORIAL SCOPE:	Austria and incidental extensions
TREATY DETAIL:	Number of Lines. 10 Gross

MAXIMUM CESSION:

ATS. 10,000,000 Sum Insured Fire or Consequential Loss.
ATS. 15,000,000 S.I. Fire and Consequential Loss Combined.

REASSURED'S MAXIMUM RETENTION:

ATS. 1,000,000 Sum Insured Fire or Consequential Loss.
ATS. 1,500,000 S.I. Fire and Consequential Loss combined.
Graded down as per Table of Limits and protected by 40% Quota Share.

RATE:	O.G.R.
COMMISSION:	Sliding Scale 25%–37.5% for Loss Ratio 60% (incurred losses/earned premium) and above to below 42%. Steps of 1.25% Commission for 2% Loss Ratio. Provisional Rate of Commission 30%. Any surplus of profit or loss above or below ratio to be carried forward for maximum of three further years.
OVER-RIDING COMMISSION:	Nil
TAXES AND OTHER CHARGES:	Fire Brigade Charges (currently 4% on O.G.R.)
BROKERAGE:	2.5% on O.G.R.
PROFIT COMMISSION:	Nil
PREMIUM RESERVE:	40%
INTEREST:	6% less tax (Current Rate 30%)
LOSS RESERVE:	Nil
PREMIUM PORTFOLIO:	35% of Gross Premium Income Ceded for the previous 12 months (Incoming and Outgoing each year).
LOSS PORTFOLIO:	90% (Incoming and Outgoing each year). Adjustable after 3 years.
PRELIMINARY LOSS ADVICE FIGURE:	ATS. 250,000
CASH LOSS:	ATS. 500,000 (for 100% of Treaty)

ACCOUNTS:	Period:	Quarterly
	Rendition:	Within 60 days
	Settlement:	Credit Balances with accounts Debit Balances within 28 days

GENERAL CONDITIONS: War and Civil War exclusion clause

WORDING: Wording to be agreed by Leading Reinsurer (R.S.T. Reinsurance Co Ltd) only

INTERNAL ARRANGEMENT: Bordereaux to be held by the Broker, B.C.D. Insurance Brokers to prepare accounts. All other documentation to be prepared by C.A.B. Insurance Brokers

INFORMATION: (1) See Questionnaire Date 20.10.84
(2) E.P.I. 1985 ATS. 7,500,000

APPENDIX 3

CATASTROPHE EXCESS OF LOSS SLIP DETAILS

REASSURED:	Splendid Insurance Company Limited
PERIOD:	12 months from 1 January 1996. Losses Occurring Basis.
TYPE:	GENERAL CATASTROPHE EXCESS OF LOSS.
CLASS:	All business written and retained net in the Reinsured's Fire, Motor and General Property Accounts.
TERRITORY:	Worldwide, excluding USA and Canada unless incidental.
LIMIT:	To pay up to US$ 50,000,000 ultimate net loss, each and every loss occurrence. Excess of US$ 32,500,000 ultimate net loss, each and every loss occurrence.
REINSTATEMENT:	One full reinstatement at 100% additional premium pro-rata to amount reinstated.
PREMIUM:	Minimum and Deposit Premium US$ 390,000 payable in four equal instalments at 1 May, 1 August, 1 November, 1996 and 1 February 1997 and adjustable on expiry at 0.225% of applicable Gross Net Premium Income.
DEDUCTIONS:	15% in all.

GENERAL CONDITIONS:	Reinsurers to have the full benefit of recoveries under specific classes excess of loss contracts (as per schedule) in force or so deemed. Net Retained Lines Clause. Extended Expiry Clause. Hours Clause: a) 72 consecutive hours as regards a cyclone, a hurricane, a typhoon, a windstorm, a rainstorm, a hailstorm and/or a tornado. b) 72 consecutive hours as regards an earthquake, a seaquake, a tidal wave and/or a volcanic eruption. c) 72 consecutive hours and within the limits of one City, Town or Village as regards riots, civil commotions and malicious damage. Currency Conversion Clause. Exclusions: 1. Obligatory Reinsurance 2. War and Civil War 3. Nuclear Energy Risks Clause (NMA 1975, 1166, 1248, 1251 and 1119).
WORDING:	As expiring as far as possible.
INFORMATION:	12 months Estimated GNPI 1996, US$ 245,000,000.

APPENDIX 4

STANDARD A4 SLIP FRONT COVER AND PAGE 1

POLICY NO.:

TREATY

<u>REINSURED:</u>

<u>TYPE</u>

<u>PERIOD</u>

FOR L.P.S.O. USE
FOR I.L.U. USE
FOR LIRMA USE

PAGE OF

POLICY NO. | REF. NO.

UNIQUE MARKET REFERENCE

SLIP REGISTRATION		
LLOYD'S	ILU	LIRMA

BINDING AUTHORITY REGISTRATION NO. & DATE

RISK CODE(S)

D.T.I. CODE | TOC TRIBUNAL

TERMS OF SETTLEMENT		
SETT. DUE DATE	DEF	ADJ
/ /		

ASSURED/ACCOUNT

ADJUST. SCHEME	
YES	NO

USB /NUS /US | COUNTRY OF ORIGIN | VAT

OVERSEAS BROKER (NAME AND ADDRESS)

CURRENCY	SIGNED LINE %	GROSS PREMIUM	
		IN ALL	WAR ONLY
TOTAL			
LLOYD'S			
ILU			
LIRMA			
OTHER COMPANIES			

FOR FUTURE USE

C.P.A.		SERIAL NO.	CERTICATE NOS.
YES	NO		

EC CCI	EC ESTABLISHMENT	EC SERVICES	EC N/A

BUREAU SCHEME NO. | BROKERS COVER NO.

WRITTEN LINES % PART OF ORDER WHOLE	ORDER	CLOSED FOR

Companies Leading Underwriters Agreement 1981 (CLUA). Leading Underwriters Agreement (NMA). Reductions in sum insured, reductions in overall rate/premium not exceeding 10%, increases in sum insured up to written lines plus 10%, increases in overall rate/premium to be agreed leading 2 reinsurers only. Agreed hold covered renewals or extensions hereon for 31 days if required on agreement of Leading Underwriter. Wordings, Schedule, Proposal Forms, Off Slips, Signing Slips and Annual Re-signing Slips, to be agreed Leading Underwriter. Agreed if required sign renewal policy/receipt without production of previous slip or policy.

APPENDIX 5

PROPERTY CATASTROPHE EXCESS OF LOSS TREATY WORDING

PROPERTY CATASTROPHE EXCESS OF LOSS TREATY WORDING: 11/91

Article 1—Business Covered (NP11)

This Agreement reinsures, subject to the exclusions as hereinafter provided, insurance and reinsurance written by the Reinsured as set out in the schedule.

Article II—Limits of Indemnity (NP21)

The Reinsurer hereby undertakes as regards its agreed share set out in the schedule to indemnify the Reinsured for that part of the ultimate net loss which exceeds the amount of the deductible set out in the schedule in respect of any one such net loss.

It is warranted that the Reinsured shall retain net for its own accounts without specific reinsurance the percentage set out in the schedule of any ultimate net loss together with the deductible set out in the schedule.

Article III—Period of Application (NP31)

This Agreement applies to the Ultimate Net Loss paid by the Reinsured in respect of business reinsured hereunder in accordance with the preceding Articles in respect of individual insured losses which occur during the period of this agreement as set out in the Schedule.

For the purpose of this Agreement an insured loss shall be deemed to occur when the loss of or damage to the original subject matter of insurance caused by the operation of an original insured peril first becomes manifest.

Article IV—Territory (NP41)

This Agreement applies to property located in territories set out in the schedule.

Article V—Exclusions

1. War and Civil War Exclusion Clause (G51)

This Agreement does not cover liability assumed by the Reinsured on loss or damage directly or indirectly occasioned by, happening through or in consequence of war, invasion, acts of foreign enemies, hostilities or war-like operations (whether war to be declared or not), civil war, mutiny, civil commotion assuming the proportions of or amounting to a popular rising, military rising, insurrection, rebellion, revolution, military or usurped power, martial law, confiscation or nationalisation or requisition or destruction of or damage to property by or under the order of any Government or public or local authority, or any act of any person or persons acting on behalf of or in connection with any organisation the objects of which are to include the overthrowing or influencing or any de jure or de facto government by terrorism or by any violent means.

. . .

3. Third Party Liability Exclusion Clause (NP53)

This Agreement shall not apply to any amount of Ultimate Net Loss which arises directly or indirectly in respect of third party liability coverage.

4. Reinsurance Exclusion Clause (NP54)

This Agreement shall not apply to any reinsurance assumed by the reinsured other than facultative and proportional reinsurance.

Article VI—Hours Clause (NP61)

For the purposes of this Agreement a loss occurrence shall consist of all individual insured losses which are the direct and immediate result of the sudden violent physical operation of one and the same manifestation of an original insured peril and occur during a loss period of 72 consecutive hours as regards any:

(a) hurricane, typhoon, windstorm, rainstorm, hailstorm or tornado
(b) earthquake, seaquake, tidal wave or volcanic eruption
(c) fire
(d) riot or civil commotion which occurs within the limits of one City, Town or Village, or
(e) 168 consecutive hours as regards all other original insured perils

It is further agreed that all individual insured losses which are the direct and immediate result of:

(i) malicious damage which occurs within the limits of one City, Town or Village during a loss period of 72 consecutive hours shall constitute an individual loss occurrence for the purposes of this Agreement as shall

(ii) any flood or floods which occur within the catchment area of any named river and its tributaries during a loss period of 168 consecutive hours. It being understood that for the purposes of this Article a flood shall mean the escape of water from its normal confines (other than tanks, apparatus, pipes and similar water containers forming part of buildings).

Provided that if any such aforementioned operation and physical manifestation shall directly and immediately result in the physical manifestation of another original insured peril or perils then all individual insured losses which directly and immediately result therefrom and occur during the same loss period of 168 consecutive hours or 72 consecutive hours where any of the perils mentioned in (a) (b) (c) and (d) above are involved shall be deemed to constitute a single loss occurrence.

The reinsured may choose the date and time when the appropriate loss period commences provided that no such period shall commence earlier than the time of the first recorded individual insured loss to which this Agreement applied resulting from the operation and manifestation of an original insured peril as aforesaid and if the operation of such a peril shall last longer than the appropriate loss period then the Reinsured may apply further appropriate loss periods in respect of the continued operation of that peril provided none of those additional periods shall overlap.

Article VIa—Winter Freeze Clause (NP63)

A loss occurrence shall consist of all individual losses which are the direct and immediate result of the escape of water or other liquids from fixed installations resulting from freezing conditions provided the said individual insured losses:

(a) Manifest themselves within an initial period of 168 consecutive hours during which the atmospheric temperature shall have naturally fallen below 0° to give an average value of accumulated degree days in excess of 15 commencing from midnight on any day selected by the Reinsured and a further period of 168 consecutive hours following on continuously from that initial period, both of which periods shall be considered to constitute a single loss period for the purposes of the Extended Expiration Clause (NP71) (Article VII).

(b) Are located within any one LIRMA/Meteorological Office zone or group of such zones which are contiguous to one another where the aforementioned atmospheric temperature shall have prevailed over the whole of any such zone or group of zones during the initial period of 168 consecutive hours selected by the Reinsured.

For the purposes of this agreement:

(1) the value of a degree day so as to obtain an average value of accumulated degree days is to be calculated in accordance with the applicable formula set out below where:
t max = Daily maximum temperature
t min = Daily minimum temperature

(a) when the maximum temperature is below freezing point the calculation is determined by the formula:

$$0 - \frac{(\text{max} + \text{t min})}{2}$$

(b) when the maximum air temperature is above freezing point, but by a lesser amount than the minimum air temperature is below freezing point, then the following formula is used:

$$\tfrac{1}{2}\,(0 - \text{t min}) - \tfrac{1}{4}\,(\text{t max} - 0)$$

(c) when the maximum air temperature is above freezing point, but by a greater amount than the minimum air temperature is below freezing point, then the following formula is used:

$$\tfrac{1}{4}\,(0 - \text{t min})$$

(2) The LIRMA/Meteorological Office zones are as set out below. Each zone consisting of the areas or localities having the postcodes as specified and as further described in The Post Office Guide 1988 Edition issued by the Royal Mail.

The Zones	Postcodes
1	AB DD EH FK IV KW KY PH TD ZE
2	DG G KA ML PA
3	BT
4	BB BL CA CH CW FY L LA LL M OL PR SK (all except SK 17 SY (15 16 17 19 20 21 22 ONLY) WA
5	BD DH DL DN HD HG HU HX LN LS NE S SR TS WF YO
6	B (all except 49 50 60 61 80 96 97 98) CV (1 to 13 inclusive) DE DY (1 to 9 inclusive) LE NG PE (all except 30 to 38 inclusive) ST TF SK 17 SY (1 to 14 inclusive) WS
7	BA (all except 12 13 14 15) BS CF DT EX LD NP PL SA SY (18 23 24 25) TA TQ TR
8	B (49 50 60 61 80 96 97 98) CV (all except 1 to 13 inclusive) DY (all except 1 to 19 inclusive) GL HP (all except 1 2 3 4 and 23) HR MK (all except 40 to 45 inclusive) NN OX RG (all except 21 to 28 inclusive) SL SN7 WR
9	AL CB CN CO HP (1 2 3 4 and 23) IP LU MK (40–45 inclusive) NR PE (30 to 38 inclusive) SG 22 WD

10	BA (12 13 14 15) BH GU (11 to 14 inclusive and 30 to 35 inclusive) PO (all except 18 to 22 inclusive) RG (21 to 28 inclusive) SN (all except 7) SO
11	BR CR DA E EC EN HA IG KT N NW RM SE SM SW TW UB W WC WD
12	BN CT GU (all except 11 to 14 inclusive and 30 to 35 inclusive) ME PO (18 to 22 inclusive) RH TN

It is further agreed that the Meteorological Office's decision as to the average value of accumulated degree days within any continuous period of 168 hours in any of the above zones or group of zones shall be final and binding on the parties for the purposes of this Agreement.

Article VII—Extended Expiration Clause (NP71)

If this Agreement shall expire while a loss period is in progress the Reinsured shall be covered hereunder in respect of all individual insured losses occurring during that loss period as if such expiration had occurred at the end of the said loss period.

Article VIII—Ultimate Net Loss Clause (NP81)

The term "ultimate net loss" shall mean the sum actually paid by the Reinsured in settlement of the individual insured losses constituting any single loss occurrence including necessary litigation and other reasonable expenses incurred by the Reinsured in connection with the adjustment thereof excluding office expenses and salaries of the Reinsured and after deduction of all salvages and recoveries including recoveries from all reinsurances insuring for the benefit hereof whether collected or not.

All salvages, recoveries or payments recovered or received subsequent to any loss settlement hereunder shall be applied as if recovered or received prior to the aforesaid settlement and all necessary adjustments shall be made by the parties hereto. Nothing in this clause shall be construed to mean that a recovery cannot be made hereunder until the Reinsured's ultimate net loss has been ascertained.

Article VIIIa—Liquidation Clause (NP83)

Notwithstanding that this Agreement constitutes an indemnity in respect of amounts actually paid by the Reinsured in accordance with the provisions of Article VIII (the Ultimate Net Loss Clause) hereof it is further agreed that in the event of the liquidation of the Reinsured on grounds of insolvency the liability of the Reinsurer shall be determined as if the Reinsured had not gone into liquidation to the extent that amounts payable by the Reinsurer shall not be reduced nor the time of their payment be delayed merely by reasons of such liquidation subject always to any rights of set-off both legal and contractual which the Reinsurer may have.

Article IX—Multiple Coverage Clause (NP91)

The Reinsurer shall be under no liability hereunder in respect of any amount of the Ultimate Net Loss which is also covered by any other reinsurance except where such liability arises under Article VII above and the other reinsurance is a renewal or replacement of this Agreement.

Article X—Reinstatement Clause (NP101)

In the event of the whole or any portion of the indemnity given hereunder being exhausted the amount so exhausted shall be automatically reinstated from the time of commencement of the appropriate loss period subject to payment of a pro-rata as to time and amount additional premium calculated on the premium due hereunder.

If the loss settlement is made prior to the adjustment of premium the reinstatement premium shall be calculated provisionally on the deposit premium subject to adjustment when the reinsurance premium hereon is finally established.

Nevertheless, the Reinsurer shall never be liable to pay more than the limit of indemnity as set out in the schedule in respect of any loss occurrence nor more than the amount set out in the schedule in all in respect of the period of this Agreement representing the number of reinstatement(s) of the limit of indemnity set out in the schedule.

Article XI—Net Retained Lines Clauses (NP111)

This Agreement shall protect only that portion of any insurance or reinsurance which the Reinsured, acting in accordance with its established practices at the time of the commencement of this Agreement, retains net for its own account. The Reinsurer's liability hereunder shall not be increased due to any error or omission which results in the Reinsured's net retention being larger than it would normally have been nor by the Reinsured's failure to reinsure and maintain reinsurance in accordance with its established practice as aforesaid, nor by the inability of the Reinsured to collect from any other reinsurers any amounts which may have become due from them for any reason whatsoever.

Article XII—Premium (NP121)

A deposit premium as set out in the schedule shall be paid by the Reinsured according to the method of payment set out in the schedule.

As soon as possible after the expiry of this Agreement the above deposit premium shall be adjusted to an amount equal to the rate set out in the schedule applied to the Reinsured's premium income as defined herein, subject to the premium set out in the schedule. The payment of any adjustment due between the parties shall thereupon become payable forthwith.

Article XIII—Premium Income (NP131)

a) Gross Premium Income (G.P.I.)

The term "premium income" shall mean the gross premium of the Reinsured in respect of the business described in Article 1 reinsured hereunder written during the period of this Agreement, less only returned premiums.

b) Gross Net Premium Income (G.N.P.I.)

The term "premium income" shall mean the gross premium of the Reinsured in respect of the business described in Article I reinsured hereunder written during the period of this Agreement, less only returned premiums and premiums paid for reinsurances entered into for the benefit of this Agreement.

c) Net Premium Income (N.P.I.)

The term "premium income" shall mean the gross premium of the Reinsured in respect of the business described in Article I reinsured hereunder written during the period of this Agreement, less commissions, premium taxes and similar deductions, brokerage and profit commission, returned premiums and premiums paid for reinsurances entered into for the benefit of this Agreement.

Article XIV—Currency Conversion (NP141)

For the purposes of this Agreement currencies other than the currency in which this Agreement is written shall be converted into that currency at the rates of exchange used in the Reinsured's books or where there is a specific remittance for a loss settlement at the rates of exchange used in making such remittance.

Article XV—Inspection of Records Clause (G151)

For as long as either party remains under any liability hereunder the Reinsured shall, upon request by the Reinsurer, make available at the Reinsured's head office or wherever the same may be located, for inspection at any reasonable time by such representatives as may be authorised by the Reinsurer for that purpose, all information relating to business reinsured hereunder in the Reinsured's possession or under its control and the said representatives may arrange for copies to be made at the Reinsurer's expense of any records containing such information as they may require.

Article XVI—Change in Law Clause (G161)

In the event of any change in the law, whether arising from legislation, decisions of the courts or otherwise, at any time after the Reinsurer entered into this Agreement by which the Reinsurer's liability hereunder is materially increased or extended the parties hereto agree to take up for immediate discussion at the request of either party a suitable revision in the terms of this Agreement. Failing agreement on such revision within thirty days after such a request it is agreed that the Reinsurer's liability hereunder whensoever arising shall be determined as if the said change in law had not taken place.

Article XVII—Underwriting Policy Clause (G171)

It is a condition precedent to the Reinsurer's liability hereunder that the Reinsured shall not introduce at any time after the Reinsured enters into this Agreement any change in its established acceptance and underwriting policy which may increase or extend the liability or exposure of the Reinsurer hereunder in respect of the classes of business to which this Agreement applies without the prior written approval to the Reinsurer.

Article XVIII—Claims Settlements Clause (NP181)

The Reinsurer shall accept all claims settlements made by the Reinsured in accordance with the terms and conditions of the business reinsured hereby to which they relate.

Article XIX—Alterations Clause (G191)

No variation in the Agreement shall be effective unless evidenced in writing and duly signed on behalf of both parties. Variations sent by instantaneous means of communication are also effective provided they are capable of being shown by means of permanent or retrievable record to have been agreed by both parties.

Article XX—Special Cancellation Clause (G201)

1. Either party shall have the right to terminate this Agreement immediately by giving the other party notice:

   a) If the performance of the whole or any part of this Agreement be prohibited or rendered impossible de jure or de facto in particular and without prejudice to the generality of the preceding words in consequence of any law or regulation which is or shall be in force in any country or territory or if any law or regulation shall prevent directly or indirectly the remittance of any payments due to or from either party.

b) If the other party has become insolvent or unable to pay its debts or has lost the whole or any part of its paid up capital or has had any authority to transact any class of business withdrawn, suspended or made conditional.
c) If there is any material change in the ownership or control of the other party.
d) If the country or territory in which the other party resides or has its head office or is incorporated shall be involved in armed hostilities with any other country whether war be declared or not or is partly or wholly occupied by another power.
e) If the other party shall have failed to comply with any of the terms and conditions of this Agreement.

After the date of any such termination the liability of the Reinsurer hereunder shall cease outright other than in respect of individual insured losses which have occurred prior hereto.

2. All notices of termination in accordance with any of the provisions of this paragraph shall be by cable telex or any other means of instantaneous communication and shall be deemed to be served upon despatch or where communications between the parties are interrupted upon attempted despatch.

3. All notices or termination served in accordance with any of the provisions of this Article shall be addressed to the party concerned at its head office or at any other address previously designated by that party.

Article XXI—Intermediaries Clause (G211)

The intermediaries named in the schedule are recognised as the intermediary negotiating this Agreement through whom all communications between the parties hereto shall be transmitted subject to the provision of Article XX, subparagraph 3 (Special Cancellation Clause).

Arbitration Agreement (G230)

1. All matters in difference between the parties in relation to the contract to which this Agreement is attached, including information and validity, and whether arising during or after the period of that contract, shall be referred to an arbitration tribunal in the manner hereinafter set out.

2. Unless the parties agree upon a single arbitrator within thirty days of one receiving a written request from them for arbitration, the claimant (the third

party requesting arbitration) shall appoint his arbitrator and give written notice thereof to the respondent. Within thirty days of receiving such notice the respondent shall appoint his arbitrator and give written notice thereof to the claimant, failing which the claimant may apply to the appointor hereinafter named to nominate an arbitrator on behalf of the respondent.

3. Before they enter upon a reference the two arbitrators shall appoint a third arbitrator. Should they fail to appoint such a third arbitrator within thirty days of the appointment of the respondent's arbitrator then either of them or either of the parties may apply to the appointor for the appointment of the third arbitrator. The three arbitrators shall decide by majority. If no majority can be reached the verdict of the third arbitrator shall prevail. He shall also act as Chairman of the Tribunal.

4. Unless the parties otherwise agree the arbitration tribunal shall consist of persons with not less than ten years' experience of insurance or reinsurance.

5. The arbitration tribunal shall have power to fix all procedural rules for the holding of the arbitration including discretionary power to make orders as to any matters which it may consider proper in the circumstances of the case with regard to pleadings, discovery, inspection of the documents, examination of witnesses and any other matter whatsoever relating to the conduct of the arbitration and may receive and act upon such evidence whether oral or written strictly admissible or not as it shall in its discretion think fit.

6. The appointor shall be the Chairman for the time being of the London Insurance and Reinsurance Market Association or if he is unable to act for any reasons such person as may be nominated by the Council of that Association.

7. All costs of the arbitration shall be at the discretion of the arbitration tribunal who may direct to and by whom and in what manner they shall be paid.

8.* The seat of the arbitration shall be in the United Kingdom and the arbitration tribunal shall apply the laws of England as the proper law of this Agreement and of the contract to which this Agreement is attached.

The award of the arbitration tribunal shall be in writing and binding upon the parties who covenant to carry out the same. If either of the parties should fail to carry out any award the other may apply for its enforcement to a court of competent jurisdiction in any territory in which the party in default is domiciled or has assets or carries on business.

* This form of agreement may be used in other territories under the appropriate local law but if the seat of arbitration is outside the United Kingdom, an alternative appointer should be nominated in paragraph 6.

EXAMPLE OF SCHEDULE

SCHEDULE ATTACHING TO AND FORMING PART OF

Name of Reinsured

Article I Business Covered:

Article II Limits of Indemnity:

Agreed share %

Limit Deductible Co-reinsurance %

Article III Period of Application:

Commencement Expiry

Article IV Territory:

Article V Exclusions:

Additional exclusions:

Article X Reinstatement Clause:

Aggregate Liability . Number of reinstatements

Article XII Premium:

Deposit Premium Minimum Premium

Method of payment of deposit premium: Payable

Article XXI Intermediaries Clause:

Name of intermediary

In witness whereof both the above written Reinsurance Agreement and the district Arbitration Agreement have been drawn up and signed on behalf of parties hereto.

For and on behalf of

in the day of 19

For and on behalf of

in the day of 19

APPENDIX 6

PROPERTY QUOTA SHARE WORDING

PROPERTY QUOTA SHARE—REINSURANCE AGREEMENT

Article I—Cession (Clause P12)

(a) The Reinsured shall reinsure by way of quota share reinsurance the proportion stated in the Schedule (hereinafter called the "Reinsurer's participation") of the business specified in the Schedule but not exceeding the treaty limit stipulated therein.

(b) The Reinsurer shall cover only those risks accepted by the Reinsured which are situated within the territorial limits as defined in the Schedule.

(c) The Reinsurer shall not be liable for any losses caused by or arising from the exclusions detailed in the Schedule.

(d) The Reinsured shall retain net its own account the share specified in the Schedule of each risk to which this Agreement relates. However, the Reinsured may in the interest of the Reinsurer reduce the amount to be ceded in respect of any risk by effecting individual reinsurances. The Reinsured may also effect reinsurance to protect its overall net retained portfolio.

(e) An insurance granted by the Reinsured wherein the Reinsured is named as the Insured either alone or jointly with another party or parties shall not be excluded from this Agreement merely because no legal liability may arise in respect thereof by reason of the fact that the Reinsured be the Insured or one of the Insureds.

(f) The liability of the Reinsurer in respect of each risk covered hereunder shall commence and expire simultaneously and automatically with the liability of the Reinsured in respect of the original acceptance subject to the provisions relating to Commencement and Termination.

Article II—Commencement and Termination (Clause P31)

(a) This Agreement shall take effect on the date stated in the Schedule and continue in force until terminated and shall be in respect of policies issued or renewed during the period of this Agreement not to exceed 12 months plus odd time, not exceeding 18 months in all.

(b) This Agreement may be terminated by either party giving notice of termination on the basis set out in the Schedule, such notice to expire on the date indicated in the Schedule. Notice of termination shall be given in writing which shall be deemed to include cable, telex, facsimile or any other means of instantaneous communication. In the event of either party giving notice of termination in accordance with the provisions set out in the Schedule then such notice shall be automatically deemed to have been given by both parties. During the period of notice the Reinsurer shall continue to participate in all cessions covered by the terms of this Agreement.

Article III—Record of Cessions and Bordereaux (Clause P16)

(a) The Reinsured shall maintain a record of all cessions hereunder and of all renewals and alterations thereto and these shall be advised as stated in the Schedule to the Reinsurer on a bordereau form.

(b) Bordereaux shall serve only to provide information to the Reinsurer in respect of risks ceded under this Agreement. Risks outside the scope of this Agreement shall not be covered by this Agreement by virtue of an entry on a bordereau form.

(c) If any inadvertent delay, error or omission shall be made in connection with the ceding of business in accordance with the provisions of this Article then, provided that full disclosure is made in writing to the Reinsurer within twelve months of the date of inception of the original policy concerned, the cession shall be deemed to have been made in due form either in accordance with the Reinsured's intent where the latter is able to furnish adequate proof thereof or, when this is not possible, then in accordance with the Reinsured's established practice in ceding business hereto.

Article IV—Change of Underwriting Policy (Clause G171)

It is a condition precedent to the Reinsurer's liability hereunder that the Reinsured shall not introduce at any time after the Reinsured enters into this Agreement any change in its established acceptance or underwriting policy which may increase or extend the liability or exposure of the Reinsurer hereunder in respect of the classes of business to which this Agreement applies without the prior written approval of the Reinsurer.

Article V—Claims Advice and Settlement (Clause P181.1)

(a) The Reinsured shall advise the Reinsurer of any claims where the share for 100% of the treaty is estimated to equal or exceed the sum stated in the Schedule or its equivalent in other currencies.

(b) All loss payments made by the Reinsured within the conditions of the business covered hereunder and falling within the scope of this Agreement shall be binding upon on the Reinsurer. The Reinsurer shall be liable for its proportion of such loss payments in respect of any risks ceded hereto less its proportion of any recoveries applicable thereto made by the Reinsured whether as salvage or otherwise. All legal costs and professional fees and expenses (excluding salaries of all employees and office expenses of the Reinsured) which are reasonably incurred in connection therewith shall form part of such loss payments.

(c) The Reinsured shall have the right to request immediate payment from the Reinsurer of the Reinsurer's proportion of any loss settlement which equals or exceeds the amount stated in the Schedule.

(d) The Reinsured shall as soon as practicable and in any event not later than at the end of each twelve month period send to the Reinsurer a statement of unsettled claims as at the date of such statement showing an amount for which the Reinsurer may be liable.

Article VI—Premium and Deductions (Clause P121)

(a) The premium due by the Reinsured to the Reinsurer shall be the Reinsurer's proportion of the original gross premium or as defined in the Schedule and hereinafter referred to as "premium" in respect of all risks ceded hereto.

(b) The Reinsurer shall allow commission on the premiums ceded in the accounts for this agreement at the rate specified in the Schedule but unless otherwise agreed and specified in the Schedule no other deduction shall be made.

Article VII—Profit Commission (Clause P241)

(a) The Reinsurer shall pay to the Reinsured a profit commission as detailed in the Schedule calculated on the profit arising from all business ceded under this Agreement and included in the accounts for each annual period of this Agreement in accordance with the following formula:

INCOME

1. Release of preceding year's Unearned Premium Reserve
2. Release of the Outstanding Loss Reserve as at the end of the preceding year
3. Premium included in the accounts for the current year.

Items 1 and 2 will not apply to the first Profit Commission Statement.

OUTGO

1. Commission included in the accounts for the current year
2. Any other agreed deductions as specified in the Schedule

3. Paid Losses and Loss Expenses included in the accounts for the current year including cash losses paid by the Reinsurer during the current year and not brought into account
4. Unearned Premium Reserve calculated on the Premium for the current year at the rate specified in the Schedule
5. The Outstanding Loss Reserve as at the end of the current year
6. Reinsurer's Management Expenses calculated on the Premium for the current year at the rate specified in the Schedule
7. Deficit (if any) brought forward from the previous year's statement.

(b) Any Premium and Loss recoveries under reinsurance which inure to the benefit of this Agreement shall be taken into consideration.

(c) Any loss resulting from each year's profit commission calculated shall be carried forward for the number of years stated in the Schedule. Within this period any loss shall be used to eliminate and/or reduce any subsequent years' profit(s) in the order in which they arise.

(d) Any excess of Income over Outgo shall be deemed to be the profit for the annual period.

(e) The Reinsured shall render to the Reinsurer a statement for each annual period in accordance with the above formula and any profit commission due shall be included in account.

(f) On termination of this Agreement no Profit Commission Statement shall be rendered until all liability of the Reinsurer has ceased. All entries appearing in accounts rendered to the Reinsurer after the date of termination together with the appropriate entries relating to the last period this Agreement was in force shall be included in the final statement.

Article VIII—Accounts (Clause P251)

(a) The accounts between the Reinsured and the Reinsurer in respect of the business under this Agreement shall be closed as stated in the Schedule and rendered in original currency by the Reinsured as soon as possible thereafter but in any event not later than two months after the end of the stated period.

(b) Accounts shall be confirmed by the Reinsurer within one month of receipt but inadvertent errors and/or omissions in the accounts shall not delay the payment of any balance due hereunder unless such errors and/or omissions have a major effect ont the remittable balance. Any necessary correction shall be made in the next account rendered hereunder except in those cases where the error and/or omission has a major effect on the remittable balance necessitating an immediate adjustment.

(c) Balances due to the Reinsurer shall be paid by the Reinsured at the same time as the accounts are rendered and balances due to the Reinsured shall be paid at the time of confirmation.

Article IX—Overdue Balances (Clause P252)

Any amounts outstanding after the date on which settlement is due should be subject to the payment of interest by the debtor. Interest shall be calculated at the rate stated in the Schedule and remain payable until the date upon which payment is received by the creditor.

Article X—Premium Reserve Deposit—(alternative 1) Cash Only (Clause P261)

(a) The Reinsured shall retain from the Reinsurer a Premium Reserve Deposit in cash calculated at the percentage stated in the Schedule on the premium ceded to the Reinsurer in the accounts rendered hereunder. Such retained Deposit shall be released to the Reinsurer in the corresponding account of the following year.

(b) The Reinsured shall credit the Reinsurer in the final account for the year with the interest accrued on the cash Deposit retained in each annual period.

(c) The annual percentage rate of interest payable is as stated in the Schedule.

(d) Alterations in the rate of interest payable at the renewal of this Agreement shall be applied to all cash Deposits in accounts rendered from the commencement of that year regardless of their underwriting year designation.

(e) Any amount held by the Reinsured in accordance with the provisions of this clause remain the property of the Reinsurer so far as the applicable Law permits and are held by the Reinsured as trustee for the Reinsurer and may only be utilised by the Reinsured in the event and up to the amount of the Reinsurer's failure to discharge its liability under this Agreement.

(f) The Reinsurer may at its discretion direct that any such amount or any portion thereof which should be released to the Reinsurer in accordance with the provisions of this clause or an amount equivalent to the value thereof shall instead be set off against any amounts owed by the Reinsurer to the Reinsured under this or any other agreements which have been or may hereafter be entered into between parties, it being understood that the Reinsurer shall relinquish to the Reinsured all its rights in the said amount to the extent of any such set-off.

Article X—Premium Reserve Deposit—(alternative 2) Cash and Securities etc. (Clause P262)

(a) The Reinsured shall retain from the Reinsurer a Premium Reserve Deposit (in cash) calculated at the percentage stated in the Schedule on the premium ceded to the Reinsurer in the accounts rendered hereunder. Such retained Deposit shall be released to the Reinsurer in the corresponding account of the following year.

(b) The Reinsurer may at any time request the release of the Premium Reserve Deposit retained in cash and its replacement with Letters of Credit, Bonds and/or Securities acceptable to both parties and the Reinsurer shall receive all dividends interest and other rights accruing thereon. When a Deposit is constituted in this manner any deficiency between the Premium Reserve Deposit required and the market value of the Bonds and/or Securities held shall be reported by the Reinsured to the Reinsurer so that the position can be corrected. Should this not be completed within 30 days from the date of the request the Reinsured shall have the right to submit an account to the Reinsurer calling for the deficiency to be made up immediately in cash; this being on the understanding that all accounts have been rendered and settled in accordance with the terms of this Agreement. Any deficiency made up in cash shall be released in the next account drawn up by the Reinsured following the rectification by the Reinsurer of the value of the Bond and/or Securities being made good.

(c) The Reinsured shall credit the Reinsurer in the accounts rendered hereunder with interest at the annual percentage rate stated in the Schedule on the amount of Premium Reserve Deposit retained in cash at any time.

(d) All sums in cash, Letters of Credit, Bonds or Securities held by the Reinsured in accordance with the provisions of this clause remain the property of the Reinsurer so far as the applicable Law permits and are held by the Reinsured as trustee for the Reinsurer and may only be utilised by the Reinsured in the event and up to the amount of the Reinsurer's failure to discharge its liability under this Agreement.

(e) The Reinsurer may at its discretion direct that any such cash, Letters of Credit, Bonds or Securities or any portion thereof which should be released to the Reinsurer in accordance with the provisions of this clause or an amount equivalent to the value thereof shall instead be set off against any amounts owed by the Reinsurer to the Reinsured under this or any other agreements which have been or may hereafter be entered into between parties, it being understood that the Reinsurer shall relinquish to the Reinsured all its rights in the said cash, Letters of Credit, Bonds or Securities to the extent of any such set-off.

Article XI—Outstanding Loss Reserve Deposit—(alternative 1) Cash Only (Clause P263)

(a) The Reinsured shall retain from the Reinsurer an Outstanding Loss Reserve Deposit in cash equal to the Reinsurer's share of all claims hereunder notified by the Reinsured and agreed by the Reinsurer and not paid as at the end of each annual period of this Agreement. The Deposit retained shall be released and a new deposit set up annually in the final account for each annual period.

(b) If on termination of this Agreement the Reinsurer remains liable for settlement of its share of all outstanding claims then in each account rendered thereafter in accordance with the provisions hereunder the Loss Reserve Deposit held by the Reinsured shall be released and a new deposit set up.

(c) The Reinsured shall credit the Reinsurer in the accounts rendered hereunder with interest at the annual percentage rate stated in the Schedule on the amount of Outstanding Loss Reserve Deposit retained in cash at any time.

(d) Alterations in the rate of interest payable at the renewal of this Agreement shall be applied to all cash Deposits in accounts rendered from the commencement of that year regardless of their underwriting year designation.

(e) Any amounts held by the Reinsured in accordance with the provisions of this clause remain the property of the Reinsurer so far as the applicable Law permits and are held by the Reinsured as trustee for the Reinsurer and may only be utilised by the Reinsured in the event and up to the amount of the Reinsurer's failure to discharge its liability under this Agreement or as stipulated in paragraph (f) hereof.

(f) In the event of the Reinsurer being requested to pay a cash loss in respect of a claim for which a loss reserve deposit has been retained the Reinsurer has the right to request settlement of the claim from the Outstanding Loss Reserve Deposit.

(g) The Reinsurer may at its discretion direct that any such amount or any portion thereof which should be released to the Reinsurer in accordance with the provisions of this clause or an amount equivalent to the value thereof shall instead be set off against any amounts owed by the Reinsurer to the Reinsured under this or any other agreements which have been or may hereafter be entered into between parties, it being understood that the Reinsurer shall relinquish to the Reinsured all its rights in the said amount to the extent of any such set-off.

Article XI—Outstanding Loss Reserve Deposit—(alternative 2) Cash and Securities etc. (Clause P264)

(a) The Reinsured shall retain from the Reinsurer an Outstanding Loss Reserve Deposit in cash equal to the Reinsurer's share of all claims hereunder notified by the Reinsured and agreed by the Reinsurer but not paid as at the end of each annual period of this Agreement. The Deposit retained shall be released and a new Deposit set up annually in the final account for each annual period.

(b) If on termination of this Agreement the Reinsurer remains liable for settlement of its share of all outstanding claims then in each account rendered thereafter in accordance with the provisions hereunder the Loss Reserve Deposit held by the Reinsured shall be released and a new Deposit set up.

(c) The Reinsurer may at any time request the release of the Outstanding Loss Reserve Deposit retained in cash and its replacement with Letters of Credit, Bonds and/or Securities acceptable to both parties and the Reinsurer shall receive all dividends interest and other rights accruing thereon. When a deposit is constituted in this manner any deficiency between the Outstanding Loss Reserve Deposit required and the market value of the Bonds and/or Securities held shall be reported by the Reinsured to the Reinsurer so that the position can be corrected. Should this not be completed within 30 days from the date of the request the Reinsured shall have the right to submit an account to the Reinsurer calling for the deficiency to be made up immediately in cash; this being on the understanding that all accounts have been rendered and settled in accordance with the terms of this Agreement. Any deficiency made up in cash shall be released in the next quarterly account drawn up by the Reinsured following the rectification by the Reinsured of the value of the Bond and/or Securities being made good.

(d) The Reinsured shall credit the Reinsurer in the accounts rendered hereunder with interest at the annual percentage rate stated in the Schedule on the amount of Outstanding Loss Reserve Deposit retained in cash at any time.

(e) Alterations in the rate of interest payable at the renewal of this Agreement shall be applied to all cash Deposits in accounts rendered from the commencement of that year regardless of their underwriting year designation.

(f) All sums in cash, Letters of Credit, Bonds or Securities held by the Reinsured in accordance with the provisions of this clause remain the property of the Reinsurer so far as the applicable Law permits and are held by the Reinsured as trustee for the Reinsurer and may only be utilised by the Reinsured in the event and up to the amount of the Reinsurer's failure to discharge its liability under this Agreement or as stipulated in paragraph (g) hereof.

(g) In the event of the Reinsurer being requested to pay a cash loss in respect of a claim for which a loss reserve deposit has been retained the Reinsurer has the right to request settlement of the claim from the Outstanding Loss Reserve Deposit.

(h) The Reinsurer may at its discretion direct that any such cash, Letters of Credit, Bonds and/or Securities or any portion thereof which should be released to the Reinsurer in accordance with the provisions of this clause or an amount equivalent to the value thereof shall instead be set off against any amounts owed by the Reinsurer to the Reinsured under this of any other agreements which have been or may hereafter be entered into between parties, it being understood that the Reinsurer shall relinquish to the Reinsured all its rights in the said cash, Letters of Credit, Bonds or Securities to the extent of any such set-off.

Article XII—Portfolio Premium and Loss Transfer (Clause P271)

(a) The Reinsurer shall assume liability for its share of all risks in force and all losses outstanding at the date of commencement of this Agreement and in consideration thereof the Reinsured shall credit the Reinsurer with:

(i) a portfolio premium assumption calculated on the total of the Reinsurer's proportion of the premium included in the accounts for the twelve months prior to the commencement of this Agreement, and

(ii) a portfolio loss assumption calculated on the Reinsured's estimate of the losses outstanding at the date of commencement of this Agreement.

(b) On termination of this Agreement, the Reinsured shall have the option to cancel the Reinsurer's liability under this Agreement in respect of its share of unexpired risks and/or losses outstanding at the date of termination by debiting the Reinsurer with:

(i) a portfolio premium withdrawal calculated on the total of the Reinsurer's proportion of the premiums included in the accounts for the last twelve months,
and

(ii) a portfolio loss withdrawal calculated on the Reinsured's estimate of the losses outstanding at the date of termination.

(c) The percentage or basis for the calculation of portfolios mentioned in (a) and (b) shall be as stated in Schedule.

(d) The Reinsured shall have the option to exclude from such transfer any loss or losses which are or may be the subject of dispute or for which the Reinsured is unable to make an acceptable estimate of the liability of the Reinsurer. Such loss or losses shall remain the liability of the Reinsurer(s) participating in the cession(s) and the Reinsurer(s) shall be kept fully informed of all developments pertaining thereto.

(e) Not later than the date of commencement of a new treaty period or prior to the date of termination of this Agreement the Reinsured must advise the Reinsurer of its intention if portfolio premium and/or loss is to be assumed or withdrawn in respect of changes in the Reinsurer's share or on termination. The Reinsured cannot effect portfolio loss withdrawal by itself without the express written agreement of the Reinsurer.

(f) If this Agreement provides for the retention of Premium Reserve Deposits the following procedure shall apply:

- (i) At commencement of this Agreement the Deposit retained shall be equal to the portfolio premium assumption which shall be released as provided in the Schedule.
- (ii) On termination of this Agreement the total Deposit retained shall be released on withdrawal of portfolio premium.
- (iii) For a portfolio premium assumption relating to an increase in share the Deposit retained shall be revalued to the new participation and released in the normal manner. Alternatively the net portfolio premium assumption may be retained to be released as provided in the Schedule.
- (iv) For a portfolio premium withdrawal relating to a decrease in share the Deposit retained shall be revalued to the new participation with the proportionate release of Deposit.

Interest at the agreed rate for Deposits as stated in the Schedule shall be payable thereon.

(g) All the accounting transactions referred to above shall be effected at the same time with the sums relating to the portfolio withdrawal included in the final account of each year. The sums relating to the portfolio assumption shall be included in a preliminary account for the following year which shall be issued simultaneously with the aforementioned account.

(h) The portfolio items shall be included in any loss ratio or profit commission calculations that may be provided for under this Agreement and reserves for unearned premiums and outstanding losses which form part of these calculations shall be revalued to take account of portfolio withdrawals at the close of the year. Portfolio assumptions having been credited in a preliminary account at the commencement of year shall be brought into the aforementioned calculations at the close of that year. For the computation of a loss ratio the portfolio premium shall be included in the Earned Premium and the portfolio loss included in the Incurred Loss.

Article XIII—Set-Off (Clause G122)

Either party may at its discretion set off against any amounts due from the other party hereunder or under any other Agreements between the parties hereto any amounts which are due under this or those other Agreements. However, it is agreed that a party will not exercise these rights unless it has grounds to serve the other party with a Notice of Termination under the Special Cancellation Clause.

Article XIV—Inspection of Records (Clause G151)

For as long as either party remains under any liability hereunder the Reinsured shall, upon request by the Reinsurer, make available at the Reinsured's Head Office or wherever the same may be located, for inspection at any reasonable time by such representatives as may be authorised by the Reinsurer for that purpose, all information relating to business reinsured hereunder in the Reinsured's possession or under its control and the said representatives may arrange for copies to be made at the Reinsured's expense of any of the records containing such information as they may require.

Article XV—Intermediaries (Clause G211)

The intermediaries named in the Schedule are recognised as the intermediary negotiating this Agreement through whom all communications between the parties hereto shall be transmitted, subject to the provision of Article XVIII Special Cancellation.

Article XVI—Alterations (Clause G191)

No variation in the Agreement shall be effective unless evidenced in writing and duly signed on behalf of both parties. Variations sent by instantaneous means of communication are also effective provided they are capable of being shown by means of permanent or retrievable record to have been agreed by both parties.

Article XVII—Change in Law (Clause G161)

In the event of any change in the law, whether arising from legislation, decisions of the courts or otherwise, at any time after the Reinsurer entered into this Agreement by which the Reinsurer's liability hereunder is materially increased or extended the parties hereto agree to take up for immediate discussion at the request of either party a suitable revision in the terms of this Agreement. Failing agreement on such revision within 30 days after such a request it is agreed that the Reinsurer's liability hereunder whensoever arising shall be determined as if the said change in law had not taken place.

Article XVIII—Special Cancellation (Clause P201)

(a) Either party shall have the right to terminate this Agreement immediately by giving the other party written notice which shall be deemed to be served upon despatch or, where communications between the parties are interrupted, upon attempted despatch where

- (i) the performance of the whole or any part of this Agreement is or becomes prohibited or rendered impossible de jure or de facto in particular and without prejudice to the generality of the preceding words in consequence of any law or regulation which is or shall be in force in any country or territory or if any law or regulation should prevent directly or indirectly the remittance of all or any part of the balance of payments due to or from the other party.
- (ii) the other party becomes insolvent or unable to pay its debts or loses the whole or any part of its paid up capital or has its authority to transact any class of insurance withdrawn, suspended or made conditional.
- (iii) there is any material change in the management, ownership or control of the other party
- (iv) the country or territory in which the other party resides or has its Head Office or is incorporated becomes involved in armed hostilities with any other country whether war be declared or not or becomes partly or wholly occupied by another power or where a state of civil war arises in that country or territory
- (v) the other party fails to comply with any of the terms and conditions of this Agreement.

For the purposes of this Clause written notice shall be deemed to include cable, telex, telefax of any other means of instantaneous communication.

(b) The Reinsurer shall (unless specifically agreed otherwise) remain liable for its share of all cessions hereunder in force on the effective date of termination until their next annual renewal date or natural expiry or for a period not exceeding 12 months plus odd time not exceeding 18 months in all.

Article XIX—Arbitration (Clause G231)

1. All matters in difference between the parties arising under, out of or in connection with this Agreement, including formation and validity, and whether arising during or after the period of this Agreement, shall be referred to an arbitration tribunal in the manner hereinafter set out.

2. Unless the parties appoint a sole arbitrator within 14 days of one receiving a written request from the other for arbitration, the claimant (the party requesting arbitration) shall appoint its arbitrator and give written notice thereof to the respondent. Within 30 days of receiving such notice the respondent shall appoint its arbitrator and given written notice thereof to the

claimant, failing which the claimant may apply to the appointor hereafter named to nominate an arbitrator on behalf of the respondent.

3. Before they enter upon a reference the two arbitrators shall appoint a third arbitrator. Should they fail to appoint such a third arbitrator within 30 days of the appointment of the respondent's arbitrator then either of them or either of the parties may apply to the appointor for the appointment of the third arbitrator. The three arbitrators shall decide by majority. If no majority can be reached the verdict of the third arbitrator shall prevail. He shall also act as chairman of the tribunal.

4. Unless the parties otherwise agree the arbitration tribunal shall consist of persons (including those who have retired) with not less than ten years' experience of insurance or reinsurance as persons engaged in the industry itself or as lawyers or other professional advisers.

5. The arbitration tribunal shall, so far as is permissible under the law and practice of the place of arbitration, have power to fix all procedural rules for the holding of the arbitration including discretionary power to make orders as to any matters which it may consider proper in the circumstances of the case with regard to pleadings, discovery, inspection of the documents, examination of witnesses and any other matter whatsoever relating to the conduct of the arbitration and may receive and act upon such evidence whether oral or written strictly admissible or not as it shall in its discretion think fit.

6. The appointor shall be the Chairman for the time being of ARIAS (UK) or, if he is unavailable or it is inappropriate for him to act for any reason, such person as may be nominated by the Committee of ARIAS (UK). If for any reason such persons decline or are unable to act, then the appointor shall be the Judge of the appropriate Courts having jurisdiction at the place of arbitration.

7. All costs of the arbitration shall be determined by the arbitration tribunal who may, taking into account the law and practice of the place of arbitration, direct to and by whom and in what manner they shall be paid.

8. The place of arbitration may be chosen by the parties, but in default of such choice, the place of arbitration shall be London, England.

9. The proper law of this Agreement shall be the law of . . . .; in default of an express choice, the proper law of this Agreement shall be the law of the country with which it is most closely connected.

10. The award of the arbitration tribunal shall be in writing and binding upon the parties who consent to carry out the same.

The Schedule together with any Appendix thereto is deemed to form an integral part of this Agreement.

IN WITNESS WHEREOF this Agreement has been signed in duplicate on behalf of and by the authority of each contracting party.

In in this day of 19

For and on behalf of

And in LONDON, ENGLAND, this day of 19

For and on behalf of

SCHEDULE EFFECTIVE DATE FROM 1 JANUARY 199X

Attaching to the PROPERTY QUOTA SHARE REINSURANCE AGREEMENT made between

and

1. REINSURER'S PARTICIPATION (Article I(a))

2. BUSINESS COVERED (Article I(a))

3. TREATY LIMITS (Article I(a))

4. TERRITORIAL LIMITS (Article I(b))

5. EXCLUSIONS (Article I(c))

6. REINSURED'S RETENTION (Article I(d))

7. COMMENCEMENT (Article II(a))

8. NOTICE OF TERMINATION (Article II(b)

9. PREMIUM BORDEREAUX (Article III)

10. LOSS BORDEREAUX (Article III)

11. PRELIMINARY LOSS ADVICE (Article V(a))

12. CASH LOSS LIMIT (Article V(c))

13.	PREMIUM AND DEDUCTIONS (Article VI)	Premium Definition Commission x% Other Deductions
14.	PROFIT COMMISSION (Article VIII)	Commission x% Other Agreed Deductions Premium Reserve x% Reinsurer's Expenses x% Losses carried forward x years
15.	ACCOUNTS (Article VIII)	
16.	OVERDUE BALANCES (Article IX)	Interest x% (x per cent) per annum
17.	PREMIUM RESERVE DEPOSIT	Interest at x% (x per cent) per annum
18.	LOSS RESERVE DEPOSIT (Article XI)	x% (x per cent). Interest at x% (x per cent) per annum
19.	PORTFOLIO TRANSFER (Article XII)	Premium Loss x% (x per cent)
20.	INTERMEDIARY (Article XV)	. . . .

IN WITNESS HEREOF this Schedule has been signed in duplicate for and on behalf of any by the authority of each contracting party.

In this day of 19

For and on behalf of

In LONDON, this day of 19

For and on behalf of

APPENDIX 7

PREAMBLE

QUOTA SHARE REINSURANCE AGREEMENT

between

(hereinafter called the "Reinsured")
of the one part

and

The Insurance or Reinsurance Companies whose names and proportion appear on the attached signing pages each for its own part and not one for the other (hereinafter called the "Reinsurer") of the other part

APPENDIX 8

ATTESTATION CLAUSE

NOW KNOW YE that We, the Reinsurers each of us to the extent of the amount/percentage underwritten by us respectively, do hereby assume the burden of the Reinsurance, and promise and bind ourselves, each for itself only and not one for the other and in respect only of the due proportion of each of us, to the Reinsured, their Executors, Administrators and Assigns, for the true performance and fulfilment of this Contract.

IN WITNESS WHEREOF the Director of Policy Signing Services of LONDON INSURANCE AND REINSURANCE MARKET ASSOCIATION ("LIRMA") has subscribed his name on behalf of each of the LIRMA Companies and (where the Companies Collective Signing Agreement ("CCSA") is being implemented) on behalf of the Leading CCSA Company which is a LIRMA Member and authorised to sign this Contract (either itself or by delegation to LIRMA) on behalf of all the other CCSA Companies.

Signed
Director of Policy Signing Services

INDEX